1

Magnetic Charisma:

How to Build Instant Rapport, Be More Likable, and Make a Memorable Impression –

Gain the IT Factor

By Patrick King
Social Interaction Specialist and
Conversation Coach
www.PatrickKingConsulting.com

Table of Contents

Foreword

When Patrick asked if I would be willing to write the foreword to his new book I was more than honored. This amazing book starts with a story about the charisma of Bill Clinton, and although I never told Patrick this, I met the President once in high school as well. The man knew how to capture an audience, and he sure knew how to shake a hand.

At that time in my life, I was struggling socially in a way that almost defies belief. I didn't make my first friend in life until I was seventeen. I was surrounded by popular kids, and I could never understand what I was doing wrong. My life changed when I met a man with charisma. I watched everything he did and emulated him.

After years of hard work, I became popular. In college, I had people ask if I was the most popular kid in high school. They had no idea that I was painfully lonely. The beauty of charisma is that people only judge you at the moment. They don't look at your past. They see how you act today and assume that you've always been charismatic.

What Patrick has done here is something special. He's broken down charisma into a scientific formula. You don't have to spend years studying and mimicking someone popular. He's done the hard work for you. I wish this book had been around when I was crying myself to sleep at fifteen. I learned how to make friends the hard way, but you don't have to.

By the end of this book, you will have the superpower of charisma. You can use it to lead a company, forge marvelous connections or simply experience the popularity you've always dreamed of. I live on a tropical island in the South Pacific. My entire business is built on networking and the ability to make connections. I leave twice a year to attend conferences, and those are the only times I meet new people each year.

Without charisma, those trips would be wasted. Instead, using the very techniques shared in this book, I forge powerful business connections - including the one who introduced me to Patrick. You might not want to run for president, but get ready to have a killer handshake and a smile that lights up a room. With *Magnetic Charisma*, you will be one step closer to taking complete control of your destiny.

Jonathan Green

Bestselling Author and The Master of My Destiny

ServeNoMaster.com

Introduction

I know it's almost a cliché at this point, but there's only been one person who has literally left me speechless from how they carried themselves. He just had that "it" factor, whatever "it" is. It's a person you've probably read about before, if you've done any type of research or reading on charisma.

Bill Clinton. Slick Willy. The 42nd President of the United States, who was perhaps best known for actions outside of his official duties.

It's no coincidence that there are literally thousands of stories similar in tenor to mine.

Here's the short version of my experience: He was making an appearance at a community center close to where I lived. I wasn't particularly interested in politics at the time, but I was interested at the prospect of meeting the President of the United States. Who wouldn't be, especially when your parents kept telling you it was a once-in-a-lifetime opportunity? It was one of the first times I'd ever seen my parents jealous of me.

After a rather standard speech about how he commiserated with and related to our community, there a meet and greet with pictures. When I got to the front of the line, I mentally told myself I wasn't going to be taken in and entranced just because he was the president. I made a resolution to not be star-struck or fawn over him just because he was another type of celebrity who was probably not even going to look me in the eye.

Well, count me wrong.

As just about everyone that met him that day could attest to, he was a damn likable and charismatic guy. Indeed, I later discovered that one of major parts of his platform was that he seemed like the "everyman" you could grab a beer with, and when I discovered he had played his saxophone on *Saturday Night Live* during his election push, it made me actively want to be his buddy.

Apparently, that was the subtle, but massive power of *magnetic charisma*. In this book, we'll break down aspects of Bill Clinton's charismatic presence, but for the time being, it's more helpful to describe how he made me feel.

Even when he was surrounded by at least 11 handlers, 12 bodyguards, and countless rabid fans, he made it seem like I was his sole focus. He ignored everyone else while I was in front of him, made strong eye contact throughout, and asked questions about my life that weren't the normal, boring interview questions. He gave me the type of *sticky* eyes that made it seem like he was engrossed in me.

And what's more — he actually seemed to care about the answers I gave, and asked questions to go deeper. He didn't just say, "Oh, that's great" or "Interesting!" like the people in my life would. I thought it would be obvious that he was preoccupied and there in body only, while mentally, he was focused on something like foreign policy. But he seemed to have a genuine fascination with my life. When I said something he agreed with, he nodded vigorously and laughed.

Did he really want to know about my dog, family,

and favorite class in school?

Probably not, but the empathy he emanated told me otherwise. It sounds like I'm describing an amazing date, and in a sense, it's not that different of a feeling.

These are subtle actions and traits that we don't fully utilize in our daily life, but the President of the United States does when he meets strangers for a split second. The fact that the singular most powerful person in the western world can make the effort really shifted my perspective on how I should interact with people.

He just made me feel good, important, and heard — the desired byproducts of charisma. Much of what creates a feeling of someone having charisma happens in the mind of the recipient, and there are many ways that you can emulate the charisma of a U.S. president.

Charisma by itself isn't a quality that is easily defined, but it's easy to define what you want from it and how you want to make others feel because of it.

You want to captivate people, become magnetic, and appear eminently likable and attractive.

Others should feel spellbound and transfixed by your presence, yet find the experience comfortable and intimate.

Magnetic Charisma is a synthesis of years of intense study, practice, teaching, and observation on the subtle ways that charismatic people act differently. Focus on the keyword "subtle" — you may be surprised at what has passed you by on a daily basis.

Chapter 1. Charisma Deconstructed

Unfortunately, charisma is seen by many people to be an immutable quality. This means that it's a "you were born with or without it" trait that people are unable to gain through practice and instruction.

Of course, I would beg to differ. These are the types of limiting, disorienting beliefs regarding charisma that not only add to its mystique, but also make it hard to develop in your own life. The Little Engine That Could thought he could, and therefore, he did. If you don't think you can, then you definitely cannot.

When I was younger, I was what you might call overweight. As a result, I was an easy target for other kids, and this combination made me extremely withdrawn and shy until my teens. The phrase "roly poly" was used more than once.

I can distinctly remember feelings of awe and jealousy when I looked at other kids who had no trouble talking to strangers and putting themselves in situations where they were essentially thinking on their feet the entire time. It seemed so impossible to me, and so out of my realm of reality that I thought you had to be born with that ability. If I was stuck at level one, it seemed out of the question to get to level 10, where they might have been born at level seven.

People are born with different skills, but let's suppose you are starting to train for a marathon. At the outset, without prior training or experience, 26.2 miles in a single run seems incredibly daunting — impossible to many. Slowly, you start with two miles a day. Then you increase your mileage to four miles a day. Eventually, you begin running over 10 miles a day and well into the teens. Suddenly, because you have applied yourself, gotten some practice, and built yourself from the ground up, 26.2 miles doesn't seem impossible. In fact, it seems entirely within your reach.

It's easy to be intimidated when we see people doing things we never think we can — working a room or captivating people with a story. But that's

18

because we haven't started training for our proverbial marathon and realized that it's an accumulation of experience, practice, and only some natural ability. Let's take this opportunity to break charisma down and define it in a way that is more manageable and helpful. The word itself comes from the Greek word *charis,* which roughly means "a gift of grace."

If you ask a hundred people to define charisma, chances are you'll have a hundred different definitions. But digging deep through those definitions, they tend to center around certain main themes.

I prefer to define it thusly:

Charisma (n): the ability to make people like you.

I like this definition because it doesn't prescribe any particular path or required set of traits. It's the simple ability to make a human being view you in a positive light and be drawn to you, in the way that only you can do.

And that's it. Don't attempt to overcomplicate it, because then you'll start to impart importance to things that simply don't matter. The person you have in your mind's eye as possessing the type of charismatic presence you want to exude simply understands people and knows how to get on their good side.

Humans avoid discomfort and seek pleasure. This is more commonly known as the *pleasure principle,* a theory put forth by Sigmund Freud. All we are doing here is capitalizing on human nature and conforming our actions to what gives people more pleasure. If given the choice, you will probably prefer to stand in front of a cupcake store versus a cow farm — that's a decision you're going to make on a number of factors, such as the smell, location, and amount of dirt.

Similarly with humans, there are a number of factors that make us want to stand closer to one person versus another. The pleasure principle is just as important when we are choosing people we want to spend time with and befriend.

Broadly speaking, author and researcher Olivia Fox Cabane has articulated four types of charisma. That same person you have in your mind's eye as the paragon of charisma likely has traits from all four types.

1. Focus charisma
2. Visionary charisma

3. Kindness charisma
4. Authority charisma

Focus charisma is when you make people feel that you are solely focused on them, and you two exist in a world of your own. There is intense attention and eye contact, and you seem to understand them innately. Picture a sympathetic therapist.

Visionary charisma is when you believe in a greater cause and can rally people to see and believe in that cause. You are an effective communicator and messenger because of your beliefs and conviction. Your confident passion is attractive. Picture Martin Luther King, Jr.

Kindness charisma is based on warmth and understanding. You make people feel like you truly care and can understand their emotions. Your empathy is attractive. People feel comfortable opening up to you because they won't be met with judgment. Picture Mother Teresa.

Authority charisma preys on our natural instinct to follow whom we perceive as powerful and in charge. You give the impression that you are infallible, have the answers, and deserve to be followed. People may not like you, but they believe in you and your ability to make good decisions and lead wisely. Picture any cult leader or charismatic dictator.

There is probably a type of charisma you feel more innately drawn to. Whichever it is, you'll learn aspects of all four types in this book and how they can work together without conflicting. We may only adhere to one definition of charisma, but this shows there are many approaches to achieving that goal, and you can find which works best for you.

What do we gain when are able to learn the elements of charisma? At first glance, it's easy to see how being better with people will benefit us.

Who wouldn't want to:

- Meet people and instantly convert them into buyers?
- Walk into a courtroom and easily persuade juries and judges regarding your case?
- Meet prospective romantic partners and get them to like you instantly?
- Be the life of the party?

But in reality, it goes far beyond that. Studies have repeatedly shown that people and relationships are the currency of happiness in our lives (Waldinger). With charisma, we gain the ability to control the amount of happiness in our lives and let people in who challenge us, make us laugh, and help us grow. We can proactively call the shots and determine our own social fate, as opposed to being stuck with toxic people who are merely there for convenience's sake.

Charisma is eminently learnable and teachable, and in many ways, it follows one of Newton's famed laws of motion: *For every action, there is an equal and opposite reaction.* That is to say that all of charisma and human interaction is a set of signals and cues that beget other signals and cues, and there is a science to deciphering which signals and cues work the most in your favor. In other words, charisma can often be simplified as a checklist of what to do at what time.

However, it will require brief forays out of your comfort zone. Even though there may be a logically easy set of procedures to follow, it's still an emotional battle to change your habits and introduce new, uncomfortable behaviors that you are not used to. I like to say that it's just a matter of using muscles that have long been dormant. It will take some time to warm them up, but it's only through practice and action that you will achieve your desired goal.

Don't despair if charisma still feels like an insurmountable obstacle that is meant for anyone but you. We've all got the same software and hardware — other people have just ben using it for years and are a bit more familiar with it. Just because you've got to play a bit of catch-up doesn't mean it's not in the cards.

Often, charismatic people are described as possessing a reality distortion field — as if they can create a new world and draw you inside it — that is separate from the rest of the world.

You might not have any grandiose ambitions regarding conquering the world or changing human destiny. But if you want to live a fuller life, if you want to attain more control over your daily set of circumstances, the power of charisma is within your grasp.

Chapter 2. Devote Your Attention

One of the building blocks of charisma is the ability to devote your full, undivided attention to someone. This is where people like Bill Clinton counterintuitively excel, because you would never expect someone of their magnitude to be so attentive and interested.

The core of devoting your attention is to *be present* with someone and *be engaged* in them, the moment, and what's happening around you. It has nothing to do with what you look like or what you're wearing. It doesn't even have anything to do with the people themselves.

It sounds so simple: If you are able to put the chatter in your brain on hold, you will be far more likable and charismatic in a heartbeat. But what does that mean — just put your phone away and nod more? Not quite.

Everybody has the ability to be completely present. It's not a question of ability; it's a question of *how* to devote your attention to people completely and the mindset that goes into that.

Let's take, for example, your favorite talk show host. My current favorite is Conan O'Brien. With a name like that, he really didn't have any choice but to be in the comedy business. The reason Conan and other talk show hosts embody devoting attention is because that's their sole job when they have a guest on their show.

He's hosting their show in a big studio with a sizeable audience, and yet when his guest sits down across the desk from him, everyone else vanishes and they are in a world of their own. That guest is the center of Conan's world, and everything for the next 10 minutes is geared toward focusing on the guest and making them feel as comfortable and welcome as possible. Further, Conan is insatiably curious about their stories and reacts to them as if they were the funniest things he has ever heard. He draws people out of their shells, and even turns more reserved guests into storytellers because he appears so interested and engaged.

You can instantly see how intense, undivided focus is more than just putting your phone away. Whether it originates from fake or real curiosity and interest, giving someone your true attention opens them up and makes them enjoy being around you. On a very basic level, it makes them feel like you care about them, and we are all too happy to engage with someone who appears to show interest in us.

Distractions

These days, it's easy to become afflicted with the fear of missing out (FOMO). FOMO is when we imagine there are so many interesting things going on in the world (typically, as presented through various social media) that we want to experience it all and are unable to focus on one thing at a time. It's rampant in modern society because we have so much access to, and so many choices for, ways to spend our time. When we talk to someone, it's considered normal to occasionally check our phones, reply to a text, or scroll through social media. FOMO is the opposite of being present, because you naturally disregard whatever or whoever is in front of your face.

Ironically, FOMO causes us to not experience anything because you are constantly vacillating between options and not devoting your attention to anything in particular.

While FOMO may be unsurprising, it is going to result in behaviors that make your inattention obvious to whoever you are speaking with, as well as make them feel like they are a consolation prize, just barely worthy of your attention. You won't ask questions, you won't follow up, you won't pay attention, you'll forget the topic of conversation, you'll give one-word answers, and you will generally send the message that you'd rather be anywhere else than speaking with that person, and that can hurt their feelings.

Imagine if Conan O'Brien was afflicted with FOMO while he had a guest on his show and was preoccupied with thoughts of Tahiti and tanned, dancing women. The interview would be fascinating, but not in a positive way.

Realize that FOMO will prevent you from enjoying any present moment because you'll be constantly comparing it to something better (which will always exist). You are letting opportunities for greatness slip by right under your nose. In addition to curiosity, a large part of charisma is to be mentally present and devoted to experiencing the life you are currently living — including the people within it.

If it's not FOMO and other current realities that are taking away attention and presence, it might be thoughts about the future. We live in a day and age where society teaches us that our happiness is located somewhere in the future, something that comes after an achievement of milestone. We need to keep planning, and can never turn out brains off because to do so would be detrimental to our ambition and goals. We're all micromanaging our lives to some degree and mentally keeping tabs on what we need to take care of.

This makes us almost uncomfortable in the present, insinuating that we should be doing anything but what we're doing at the moment. But once we get closer to that future state, the goal post is always moved several yards forward. It never ends, and you are never actually in the present. You're like a horse with a carrot dangling in front of it. It doesn't matter how far you run, you're still the same distance from the carrot.

Of course, focusing on your future is again the opposite of being present. Tolerate and accept the here and now. Embrace it for what it is — a moment that you will never get back, one that is sorely wasted if you are not present for it.

The final cause for distraction is the fact that we are often processing conversations in two ways simultaneously. If we are at all unsure or anxious about how we are coming off to people, we will be simultaneously trying to (1) listen to a conversation and focus on the other person, and (2) thinking of what to say and how to respond. We are thinking in two directions, which makes focus and attention impossible.

If FOMO or the future utilizes 20% of your brain power, that's 20% less you're spending on the person in front of you, and it means you are 20% less observant, sharp, quick, witty, and engaging. Your questions and answers will be 20% worse, and your stories will be 20% less interesting. You'll spot 20% less social cues and miss 20% of the hints people are giving you. If you are putting a puzzle together, you are missing 20% of the pieces.

Recall that charisma is about making people like you. The simple truth is that we don't like people who are otherwise preoccupied and make us feel small. Attention and focus shows we care.

Show That You Are Affected

Now that we understand that full attention is necessary for charisma, it's a matter of showing it to others.

Show that you are affected and impacted by what they say *non-verbally*.

Use eye contact correctly and optimally.

When someone is speaking, look into their eyes 80% of the time, and when you are speaking, look into their eyes 50% of the time. This encompasses a perfect ratio where it seems that you are engaged, but not invasive nor distant. More eye contact is not necessarily better. The more you use without a break, the more uncomfortable you will make someone.

Studies have shown there are between four and six distinct human emotions: happiness, sadness, fear, anger, surprise, and disgust (Jack, 2014). Do your eyes look the same when you experience or try to express each of these emotions? Park yourself in a front of a mirror and try it out. If you maintain the same expression for all of these emotions, expect that others will assume that you don't understand what they are saying.

For instance, are your eyes the same when you watch a car accident as when you watch puppies playing in a meadow? Also imagine the difference between how a television news anchor looks at the teleprompter, and how your eyes appear while crying at a romantic comedy.

Eye contact is a curious thing because studies have shown that those who use it are universally seen as more confident, trustworthy, and honest. We know this to be not necessarily true, so eye contact is really about appearances and perception. Achieve it and be more charismatic.

Bypass it and give into the temptation of scanning the room behind people, and people will know that you're only half there and looking for a better option.

Nod much more often.

Simply looking somebody in the eye opens the door to deeper levels of intimacy. However, it cannot exist in a vacuum. A charismatic presence is the result of a combination of a wide range of consistent signals that you project.

One of the clearest signals of attention you can send is to simply nod more. Nod while people are talking and after they finish. Give the appearance that you are focused on their information, soaking it up, and processing it.

As with eye contact, there are better and worse ways to engage in the simple act of nodding.

If you nod too quickly and too frequently, you will look like you are an overeager bobblehead on the dashboard of a car. Nodding, in this instance, is not a reaction to what's being said, but rather a habit — and people can tell the difference. More nodding is not better because then it completely robs the act of its meaning. It's like liberally using the word "love" — it means much less if you use it constantly, versus when you use it only in certain circumstances.

Therefore, use nodding as a non-verbal punctuation by (1) nodding slowly, because it gives the impression that information is literally entering your brain, and by (2) nodding at only the appropriate times when someone is speaking.

For example, when you slowly nod while someone is emphasizing a point, wants confirmation, is explaining something, or conveying an emotion, you are non-verbally saying "Yes, I understand you!" Let them know you are on the same page as them.

Follow Up

There are many aspects of devoting your full attention to someone — we've covered curiosity, resisting being preoccupied, clearing your mind, and non-verbal displays of presence. These are what will make the biggest difference in the smallest amount of time.

The last part I want to cover about devoting your attention is *following up*.

A lot of people talk, but they really are not talking to or hearing each other. They're talking to what that person represents. They just talk and wait for their turn to speak while pretending to listen, not bothering to truly hone in and listen to the other person. In other words, it's all about you.

Does that describe you? Following up is the art of asking question after question of people — and disregarding what you want to say and focusing on their topic or thoughts. Following up is the opposite of waiting for your turn to speak — you are encouraging *them* to speak with questions that seek information.

Let's think back to how Conan does it. As the host, he is almost like a job interviewer, and 90% of the conversation is him asking questions that allow his guests to be clever or clarify what they said.

This is one of the easiest ways to show people that you are with them mentally, or at least attempting to be. If you ask questions that clarify what the other person was talking about, it instantly shows that you are engaged in the conversation and care about its outcome.

You might think you are doing this, and you might occasionally. But how many questions deep will you go into a topic? One? Two? That's not a sufficient follow up — those are just questions you ask out of plain ol' courtesy. When you find yourself asking at least six questions on the same topic, now that's truly following up and showing an interest in someone else's train of thought.

In a sense, it's a selfless act. We all want to share, and you are letting someone else share more. This is a step most people don't take in normal conversations because it's just not how we are wired.

Here are some examples of questions that show that you are really listening and present.

- Really?
- Why did you think that was?
- It sounds like you're saying ...
- Can you clarify that for me?
- So for example ...
- So you're saying ...
- Can you tell me more about that?

Notice how all of these questions are easy, short, and don't require much work on your part. For many, you're just parroting the other person's words! Yet they compel the other person to speak because you are seeking their guidance and expertise, as well as showing an active interest in what they are saying.

Let's suppose I just told you about my weekend full of skiing shenanigans, and then you immediately changed the topic to the political news of the day. That's a fairly obvious sign that you don't care about anything I just said, because you moved on from it immediately. If you had asked me one or two questions about it, I might feel better. But if you had asked me five questions about my weekend of skiing, it would be pretty clear that you were interested in *me*.

Following up is a big step in appearing present because of how it causes someone to perceive you. Unfortunately, if you're trying to think of your next clarifying question while the other person is talking, they will quickly notice that you haven't paid attention to them at all.

Devoting your full attention, or at least appearing that you are fully present and invested in people, will make them feel incredibly special and valued. Suffice it to say, charisma is largely about how good you can make others feel. Attention is validation.

Dale Carnegie said it best — "You can make more friends in two months by becoming truly interested in other people than you can in two years by trying to get other people interested in you."

Chapter 3. Show Your Confidence

Charisma isn't just predicated on being present and paying full attention to someone. I would consider those things the door that you must walk through to be considered charismatic.

If charisma was determined solely by full attention and focus, however, then in theory, homeless people who follow you down the street as they interrogate you would be charismatic. That's just not the case.

Think about the people who we typically consider charismatic.

There's an unspoken element of status there — they appear to have high status, a certain amount of power, and influence over others. They may not be CEOs or managers, but they carry themselves like one. It's also somewhat circular reasoning. Are they charismatic because they have power, or are they powerful because they are charismatic?

Whatever the case, it's clear that appearing confident, high-status, and powerful are closely tied to charisma. It's as simple as the following: Do you feel more special when someone powerful is focused on you, or when a restaurant busboy is focused on you? Do you feel more important when the chancellor of your school commends you, or the janitor? Are you more easily charmed by an oil tycoon, or someone who operates an oil rig?

When someone with perceived confidence and power takes notice, it makes you feel special, because there are more reasons than not to ignore you. This is undoubtedly part of Bill Clinton's charisma — he was by all accounts the most powerful man in the world, and yet he took his time to pay full attention to a normal citizen.

The amount of confidence and power we perceive someone to have plays a huge role in how we feel about someone, and how we feel about their attention. We feel lucky to have it, we like them more, and we value it more. Our opinions will generally be higher about them simply because of their perceived confidence and power — and how we think other people perceive them, as well.

This chapter is about learning how to create the perception of confidence and power, and you're not out of luck if you aren't actually in a position of power. Power comes in many forms, and can be defined in even more ways.

The most basic view of power is that you have the clear ability to alter the world to your favor. Again, does Bill Clinton or a busboy have more ability to alter the world? This kind of power can be granted through titles, salaries, or positions. It may or may not be the most significant variety, but it's not something we can all possess.

Power comes from the way you carry yourself, how you respond to people, and how much self-confidence you possess.

In other words, you don't need to be rich to be perceived as powerful, as long as people sense that money isn't an issue and you have the ability to make things happen, regardless of your financial resources. You don't have to be built like the Austrian Oak (Arnold Schwarzenegger) to give people the impression that you are physically powerful, as long as people perceive you to have the ability to take care of physical issues and acts.

An integral component of being charismatic is to be able to demonstrate your confidence to others. The simple truth is that when we appear confident, we are more attractive and draw people to us. The converse is also true: When we appear to lack confidence, we make people uncomfortable and repel them.

Perceptions of power are exactly that — perceptions. And whenever we're talking about perceptions, it's not what you actually have, but what people around you think you have. The good news is that you only need to appeal to their perception to maintain it. If you carry yourself in the correct way and display self-confidence, people will more than gladly project power onto you.

This is all a lengthy way of saying that there are many ways of appearing like someone worth people's time, and most of them are things you can generate yourself.

Self-Confidence

One of the clearest and unmistakable signals of power is confidence.

Where does confidence come from? It's not your last name. It's not how much money you have in the bank. It's not who your parents are. Confidence is the belief that no matter what comes your way, you will be able to handle it in one way or another — and accept the outcome.

Confidence exists in many contexts and isn't always a universal sense of self.

If you are a confident basketball player, you believe that you will be able to do something when you get the ball, no matter the situation. However, if you fail to score, you accept that outcome because failure is an inevitable part of life. If you are a confident musician, you believe you will be able to perform a new piece of music at a recital, even if it's difficult. If you are confident with people, you will feel just fine being thrown into a networking event full of strangers, and be okay with the fact that not everyone will be your friend afterwards.

Confidence is a much bigger topic, so I will provide a quick primer on achieving confidence as a means to increased charisma.

First, you are probably excellent and possess

mastery over many more things than you realize. This, by itself, is cause for confidence. Everyone has something that they are the best in the world at. Take a moment to shed your modesty filter and think about what you're objectively better at compared to most people.

What were the steps required to reach that stage? Regardless of what you're good at, you likely went through a difficult process to arrive at your state of mastery and expertise. Nothing is too trivial to overlook here. You've finished a path that not many people have even begun.

Second, the narrative you tell yourself *about yourself* is likely wrong.

It's likely full of limiting beliefs that begin with "I can't, because ..." or "I would, but ..." It is full of overblown negative consequences, risks, and fears because you have constantly rationalized them to yourself and ignored evidence that says otherwise based on a gut feeling. Logically, you might know your narrative is incorrect, but internalizing that knowledge emotionally is a much bigger challenge. For instance, if you are great at soccer, but you never try out for the school team because you always tell yourself you are going to fail, that's a narrative that is fraught with assumptions and limiting beliefs.

Third, since the lack of confidence is an emotional roadblock, you are going to need an exponential amount of evidence to counterbalance it. Again, it's one thing to *know* something, and it's another to *feel* it. Emotions highly outweigh logic.

In other words, 10 pieces of positive feedback has about the same impact as one piece of negative feedback. Unfortunately, it's highly unlikely that you actually record any of the feedback you might get, which means you will only remember the negative, embarrassing moments because they tend to stick out. Thus, start recording all of your positive feedback and review it periodically to change your narrative.

Going with the same example of the soccer player, a way to record positive moments would be to take note of every good pass and shot you took, and not just the passes you bobbled or missed. You just might be surprised by how many positives there are. Any time you are in doubt, you can literally look at your feedback records to see that you are indeed a great soccer player, or more on topic, a charming person who people tend to like.

Knowledge

Another component of appearing powerful is appearing intelligent. Intelligence can serve as a proxy for education and schooling, which many project power onto. We see people who know very little as innately below us; we see those who know the same amount on the same level as us; and we see those who appear to know more than us as powerful and above us. Obviously, you should strive to know more than others.

The more you know, the more powerful you will appear. It's a signal that people will read power from. Intelligence is a widely recognized marker for status and power.

It is obviously impossible to know more than people on a consistent basis, if you're not Albert Einstein or a *Jeopardy!* champion, but aiming for a wide breadth of knowledge is as close as you can get. This type of knowledge may make have people think that you are an expert, even though it's the complete opposite of the traditional definition of an expert.

What does this mean?

Know a little bit about a lot. Eschew deep domain

expertise — in circuitry, for example — for varied knowledge in 10 other topics. This way, you'll have at least a passing familiarity with just about anything that will come up in conversation, and you will appear knowledgeable and intelligent. If you are banking on the one topic you are an expert in to come up, it's a losing proposition, and you are unnecessarily blinding yourself to the wonders of the world.

Luckily, it's also easier to gain a dearth of knowledge versus deep domain knowledge. You don't have to know everything, but you should have a passing knowledge of everything you feel might come up in conversation.

Read, read, read, and then read some more. Read about current events, read about sports, and read about topics that are specific to the contexts you will find yourself in. The fact is that a breadth of knowledge makes you appear intelligent, worldly, educated, well-read, well-traveled … you name it. It also allows you to connect with people in some way on the vast majority of their interests.

If your knowledge is spread out and impacts a wide variety of interests, people will be able to find common ground with you. Little do they know they've tapped all you know about a certain topic!

This makes people feel that they learn something new when they talk to you. It's a big part of why we all viewed our teachers and professors as so powerful when we were younger. You're engaged in seemingly intelligent conversation where you are simply bouncing around the ideas that the people you're talking to already have.

Realistically, people are not going to respect the person who is an expert on soil and worms, versus the person who has a wide breadth of knowledge and who knows something about everyone's favorite hobby. Here's the thing with narrow-focused expertise: People aren't going to relate to you if your academic and intellectual specialty is so specific and so focused that they simply can't get to your mindspace. Sometimes, it's essentially a big "who cares?" to them if you're a deep expert.

You can look very intelligent and powerful if you simply know how to ask the right questions along with that breadth of knowledge.

Body Language

To appear powerful and confident to people, it's

not a matter of telling them, "I am confident and powerful." They have to be able to see it and sense it without you saying a word, which of course leads to body language and non-verbal communication. Having confident, powerful, and strong body language makes people respect you, as well as like you. Body language has been reported to make up anywhere from 60-93% of all communication between humans, so even if you don't open your mouth, you are conveying a message about who you are just based on how you carry yourself.

If you look and walk the part, people will often assume you are more than you say and express surprise when you show vulnerability. Body language, again, is another topic that could take hours and entire books to explain, so I will try to condense this into two primary points.

First, don't be bashful in taking up space with your body.

In fact, take up more space than you currently are by making sure your chin is up, your neck is uncovered, your shoulders are stretched back, and your chest is puffed out. Pull your shoulder blades together in back. This is how you might pose when you think you are imitating a model, but it's actually the hallmark of powerfully confident posture. If it sounds like you would look like you are giving a speech to people, that's accurate. That's the way you should present yourself on a daily basis.

Now imagine your body posture when you are freezing. You are hunched over, protecting yourself, and curled into as small a space as possible to preserve body heat. That's the opposite of taking space with your body, and in any other context besides the edge of freezing, will look very meek and anxious. Slouching appears unconfident, at best.

Second, avoid nervous behaviors such as fidgeting, protecting your face and neck, shifting your weight from foot to foot, or slumping over and hiding behind handheld objects or fixtures in the room.

If you are striving to put something between you and other people, it's a clear sign of discomfort and wanting protection. These are all manifestations of subconscious insecurities or lack of confidence.

Moreover, these are all dead giveaways that you are uncomfortable in your environment, with the topic, or with yourself. And when people see that you are uncomfortable, it makes them uncomfortable. Not quite the feeling you want to evoke when you are trying to be charismatic, right?

These two body language tactics will, at the very least, make your body language neutral and not negative. Sometimes, that's enough, and more important than being absolutely charming.

Overall, you are exuding comfort and control over your environment. Recall that power is the ability to change and affect things, so appearing strong and powerful absolutely leads to that. People can literally see your power.

Speak With Authority

At first glance, this is similar to how we think about body language and posture. You are trying to take up aural space in conversation.

The parallels are actually very clear — what are the equivalents of taking up space in a conversation? It's not actually about monopolizing the conversation and talking at all times.

Speak more slowly, and perhaps more scarcely. Speak from your diaphragm clearly and powerfully — and at a volume where no one will have to ask you to repeat yourself. Create the perception that you have carefully weighed your words before you speak them, and that they carry significance. Take your time, and become comfortable with pauses and silences. Don't always rush to fill them, because that looks anxious and unconfident. It's not silence; it's just space for you to think and compose your thoughts. You'll notice others will feel supremely uncomfortable with silences and will rush to fill them.

People who are weak and insecure tend to feel compelled to interact with their environment by verbally throwing spaghetti at the wall. In other words, they keep chattering in an attempt to capture people's attention. It seems like literally every sentence is a Hail Mary from these people. After a while, it starts to reek of desperation.

The opposite of this is somebody who speaks very little, but when they do speak, they speak slowly and in a measured manner. You aren't out to impress anyone, so don't act like it.

The subconscious meaning of these actions is that

your words count. You're not the type of person who is going to open their mouth to try to placate others or put on a show. When you speak, something will happen. When you speak, you speak with power. Speaking slowly tends to amplify this effect, and people tend to listen.

Power isn't financial, nor is it tied to authority or position. The truth is people respect and aspire to those with power, and there are many ways you can create a sense of personal power around you to become more charismatic.

Chapter 4. Exude True Warmth

At first glance, it might seem like demonstrating *warmth* is virtually the same as devoting your full attention to someone.

They are similar in that they attempt to place you in the mindset of putting the other person first, second, and third in the interaction. But someone who interrogates you could be said to pay attention to you, and we don't consider that charismatic or attractive in the least. It's because it lacks the component of warmth.

Attention and focus without a warm, emotional element just becomes a job interview. It's cold, clinical, and can make people uncomfortable.

But when you combine attention with warmth and empathy, you become someone who just seems to *care deeply* about the people they come across. As you've read in the chapter about devoting your attention, it's not about altering your personality and patronizing people — it's just about small behavioral changes and moments to focus on.

Generally, showing warmth is when people feel that you are approachable, caring, empathetic, and non-judgmental. They will feel that you care about them, and they feel like you have an interest in their happiness. They feel comfortable and at ease when you're with them. It's what we typically reserve for our inner circle of family and friends, because we feel that it takes more effort to project, and we don't want to invest extra effort in strangers or mere acquaintances.

You might picture warmth as extra attention, questions, smiles, and hugs — it *is* those things, but that's just the tip of the iceberg. *True* warmth stems from a complex understanding of people and the ability to deeply empathize. It's true that it can be more effort to externally project warmth, but training empathy will make you more naturally warm out of understanding and habit.

Fabricated warmth will make you appear to be a used car salesman who calls people "buddy" in a shallow attempt to connect, whereas true warmth that stems from empathy is like speaking to a nurse with the greatest bedside manner. Since most people view warmth as something they have to put on, artificially create, and fake, they won't make the effort with most of the people in their lives. Gaining the skill of true warmth through empathy will help you stand out immensely.

The question quickly turns from how to project artificial warmth to how to actually care more about people and develop your sense of empathy. Empathy is all about putting yourself in the shoes of other people. Whenever you say something, think of how it's received by the person you're saying it to. Imagine yourself perceiving what they're perceiving, feeling what they're feeling, and really draw your heart closer to them.

Empathy

Empathy isn't naturally easy because humans are self-absorbed beings. If you strip the human condition of all societal pretense, it all boils down to selfishness. Thinking about ourselves and our priorities was an evolutionary advantage.

But even back in caveman days, we extended our empathy to our immediate family, relatives, close friends, and even other tribes, at times. Indeed, this is still the easiest way to practice the skill of empathy. We treat our immediate family differently because we care more about them. We feel defensive of them, we want the best for them, and we often think about how we can improve their lives. You know what affects them, and what makes them happy.

You could probably write a comprehensive list of thoughts and questions you have about your immediate family members that you don't have with strangers, acquaintances, or coworkers. That's where the empathy gap lies — just as you would care about an immediate family member, develop a way of caring, at least a tiny sliver, for other people like they are members of your family.

You might not *truly* care if your classmate or coworker loses his job, but what if your father loses his job? In the latter scenario, you would instantly begin to think about all of the negative consequences, how it could affect an entire group of people, and the mental anguish they must be suffering.

You might be surprised as to how quickly your sense of empathy grows if you assume a genetic and familial connection with people around you.

It's tough to not be warm and automatically care in this frame of mind.

Empathy is the ability to see life from other perspectives and feel a fraction of the emotions involved. It's not likely that you will fully understand, but substituting other people's plights with your family members' plights is sometimes as close as you can get. Indeed, a 2013 study from the University of Virginia showed that our brains react in the exact same way if a close friend is threatened as when the self is threatened — meaning the brain sees friends and family as an extension of the self, and inherently feels the pain or joy of people we are close to.

Related to this ability to see close friends as extensions of the self, search for the commonalities and similarities you have with strangers. The more you have in common, the more you will be able to relate to them, and actually care about them. In fact, this is what we unconsciously do whenever we engage in small-talk:

"I'm from Bethlehem."

"You are?! I know one person named Jim from Bethlehem ... do you know him?"

"Um … no."

We instinctually root around for commonalities as a means of building rapport. Doing so more consciously will greatly improve your sense of empathy, because people will appear to be versions of yourself.

Facetime

Another simple and powerful way to boost your sense of empathy is to deal with people on a face-to-face basis as much as possible. I know this might seem dated in the age of Facebook and Skype, and the fact that there is a greater than 50% chance you are reading this book on something that allows you to avoid face-to-face communication, but let's keep convenience out of this.

Sometimes we might have the best intentions in the world and we are sensitive to people's emotions, but we just might not catch them. The signs can be in front of our faces, but because we don't know what to look for, we don't see the subtle signs that actually tell us how people are feeling, despite the words coming out of their mouths.

If you are emailing or chatting online with someone and they tell you they lost their job, you are probably going to know how they feel and how you should react to the news. It can be very clear and obvious, until it isn't. For example:

- If they use vague language and emoticons to insist that they feel okay with losing their job, are they telling the truth?
- Something less obviously negative than losing a job is affecting them, but you have no way of knowing that it would.

Those two scenarios are just a drop in the bucket when it comes to how communicating through a screen will fail you. A smiley face doesn't really tell the whole story, does it?

Whether it's your tablet, your phone, or your laptop, there's something missing when you communicate with people without seeing them. The soul of interpersonal connection is being stripped naked. When you deal with somebody on a face-to-face basis, you gain a three-dimensional reading and surround sound perception of their tone of voice, their demeanor, their facial expression, and their *vibe*.

It's almost impossible to detect all these signals through a screen. And this is why, according to recent studies, contemporary college studies have 40% less empathy than their counterparts did 30 years ago (Twenge). It's easy to see why.

If you want to become charismatic and project true warmth, you need to put yourself in situations where you can *practice* empathy. Pick up the phone instead of texting. Make plans solely to see people and to catch up more frequently. Realize that you are not only strengthening your relationships, but improving your ability to read and feel people's emotions.

Read

Another effective way to boost your empathy levels is to read more fiction.

Here's the way fiction works: Feelings are never outright said. They are described in detail, and we encounter many situations that cause our protagonist distress or joy. But the feelings are never named, so how do we know what they are feeling? Well, we learn by their subsequent actions and thoughts. They may be heavily implied based on the internal monologues of the characters, or by how they respond to people —

but it would be a sin of storytelling to outright state the emotions frequently.

When you read more fiction, you begin to realize that it's all about getting into the heads of the characters. That's because that's where all the good stuff happens — you find motivation, emotion, and reasons for all of their actions that shape the story.

This is very easy to translate to people you talk to. As with fictional characters, your first instinct would be to look past their actions and words and think about their motivations, instead. This would include stepping into their shoes, which is a state of mind that is practiced by reading fiction.

Visualize Alternate Lives

Author George Orwell is famous for many things, most notably his novel *1984*, which was about a dystopian future.

However, what most people do not know about Orwell is that he spent roughly a year living in the poor areas of London and Paris, performing manual labor in kitchens for income, and immersing himself with the purpose of learning from his experiences. He dressed and lived the part, and recorded his learnings in a subsequent book called *Down and Out in Paris and London*. Orwell originally went in with the intent of exploring why people were poor, destitute, or homeless, and he quickly realized that it wasn't because they were all drunk or lazy. They had very real problems, and Orwell eventually became known for his involvement in social justice and inequality rights.

Now, that's the ultimate case of empathy — going undercover and living among a group of people for a year just so you can understand them. I'm not advocating that, but I am advocating that you go through the mental exercise of visualizing alternate lives and existences just like Orwell explored.

In this case, visualization isn't just thinking about how boring or cold life must be on the street; it's really going through the process of imagining how they feel when they wake up, how hungry they must be every moment of their life, how thankful they are when they receive donations, and the shame they must feel as they push their dignity aside to beg. Alcohol is also a magnificent coping mechanism that allows them to avoid the realities of daily life and numb some of the pain, and they don't know any other way to cope.

You also come to the realization that nearly everyone is just trying to do the best with what they have.

A thorough visualization of people will allow you to step inside their heads and understand them better, especially if you focus on the emotions they are feeling and where they come from.

For example, it's easy to get annoyed at somebody who bullies you, and even easier to write them off as simply being a jerk. However, if you visualize an alternate life and gain an explanation as to why they act the way they do, you'd be surprised as to how empathetic you would feel. One of the most common ways to do this is to look at that schoolyard bully and read into his story of an abusive childhood.

Maybe he was lonely when he was growing up, and this is the only way he can establish some sort of power over his life. Of course, it's anybody's guess whether this is real or not. What matters is that you are able to visualize an alternate life. This can help you develop a deep and profound sense of empathy.

If you are able to step into the shoes of people

you'd rather knock out, beat up, or dismiss, then this would enable you to become even warmer to people who treat you well.

Remember, expressing warmth to people isn't something that is done superficially. True warmth comes from understanding and empathy.

Chapter 5. Choose a Role Model

No matter how charismatic or charming you feel you are, you probably started with a role model in mind — even just a general picture of who you wanted to be. I make no secret of the fact that I treat Will Smith's character from *The Fresh Prince of Bel Air* as my role model. *The Fresh Prince of Bel Air* was a television show that ran from 1990-1996 and lives on through constant reruns.

Seeing that show and the main character was one of the first instances where I took notice of how someone interacted differently with people, and I wanted to create that feeling too.

So why the Fresh Prince?

To me, he is simply the epitome of a charismatic personality.

He says what he wants, is amazingly likeable, is comfortable being the center of attention, is confident to the point of being arrogant, can verbally spar with anyone, and flat-out hilarious. Because of how much people like him and his presence, he gets away with far more than he should be able to, and can generally use charm to shape his life.

It was amazing. Of course, I knew it was a television show and people were scripted to react to him with positivity, but you can give the same script to 100 people and 99 of them won't come close to the delivery and presence Will Smith had. Again, I knew it was a television show, but it still felt realistic in how charisma like that would affect people in a positive manner.

When I was first starting to diligently figure out the kind of person I wanted to evolve into, the Fresh Prince was an important concept for me. Since he embodied many of the things I wanted, I was able to grow, albeit sometimes in a forced and artificial way, closer to my personal ideal simply by asking myself one question:

What would the Fresh Prince do?

Earlier, we asked how Conan O'Brien (or your

favorite talk show host) would act in situations to grow your sense of curiosity. Here, you can ask what your charismatic role model would do in any social situation. You might feel like you are doing a pale imitation at first, but soon you will find your true voice as a synthesis of your personality and what elements from your role model suit you — that's why this chapter is about finding *your* role model, and not just using mine.

Putting yourself in someone's shoes has a surprising amount of benefits for growing your sense of charisma. It's a powerful question to ask yourself for a few reasons.

First, asking what your role model would do in that particular social situation diverts your attention from the situation at hand.

When we are too focused on a situation, it is too personal, or we are too invested, it suddenly becomes very difficult to make a decision because the stakes seem so high and the consequences seem so large. For example, it's near-impossible for us to abide by the amazing advice we dole out to our friends because we can't assess our own situations objectively. It's far easier to give advice, act, and even be charismatic when we are detached from the outcome and can think about it without fear or anxiety playing a part.

In other words, when you divert your attention from yourself and onto your role model, you remove a lot of the social pressure that keeps you from saying what you really want to, or acting in a way that you are scared to. Viewing social situations through an objective, relatively impersonal perspective by framing it through someone else will allow you to analyze the social situation you are in and calibrate your next move.

The more you ask yourself this question, the more habitual and second nature it will become, which is positive because you will essentially be able to condition yourself in the heat of the moment to act reflexively.

Second, having a charisma role model (or three) in mind allows you to understand how you actually want to be.

For instance, perhaps you want to develop more confidence and be more outspoken in social situations. In that case, you might ask yourself what someone like Robert Downey, Jr. would do. For another trait you want to develop — for example, a razor-sharp sense of wit and humor — perhaps you could ask yourself what Conan

O'Brien would do.

Everyone has different strengths and weaknesses, and has a different conception of how they want to be perceived. Not everyone fits the extrovert ideal of magnetic charisma, and that's perfectly fine. Not everyone wants to fit that ideal, either. So, who fits you best in terms of what you aspire to?

Men: Tyler Durden, Don Draper, Charles Xavier, Jack Donaghy, Ari Gold, John Wayne.

Women: Sheryl Sandberg, Jennifer Lawrence, Michelle Obama, Hilary Clinton, Sarah Silverman, Tina Fey.

The list could go on forever because we are not all looking for the same thing. But the act of going through this exercise should inform you as to what you feel your weaknesses are, the ways you want to be perceived, and what you ultimately feel you are missing. Get the feeling and essence of the person and how they work on the inside, rather than imitating their exact behaviors.

I would encourage you to choose a handful of role models for charisma, and then list out three specific traits you like from each of them. For instance, Robert Downey Jr.: (1) witty, (2) irreverent, and (3) brutally confident. Most of our charismatic role models will have quite a lot in common with each other, and it will allow you to see the traits that you are really chasing.

This chapter is about choosing people that excel in areas that you currently do not, and embodying them to make their reactions your habits.

Third, getting into the habit of asking what your role model would do is like donning a mask or playing a role. If you've ever acted on stage, in front of a camera, or even dressed up for Halloween, you may have noticed how differently you feel. You're not quite yourself, and that is an extremely empowering feeling.

When you're not yourself and are immersed in a mask or role, you can say and think things that you wouldn't dare to otherwise. This happens because you are literally thinking through another perspective and becoming detached from yours, and also because you know in the back of your mind that you are safe from repercussions. There's a reason that Halloween is associated with pranks, riots, and crime — because people relish the fact that they are in different roles and can do things they've always wanted to without consequence.

You feel safe, you feel empowered, and you feel confident, because it's not necessarily you that you are channeling; it's your role model.

Pick a few difficult or confusing situations you may have stuck in your head from the past few weeks. What did you do? Now, how would your role model have responded, instead? Document these, rehearse them mentally, and run through them periodically so you are able to start *thinking* like your role model instead of just emulating them. There's a big difference, isn't there? Logically, after the fact, you are able to come up with these differences, but again, it's difficult to fight against your emotions and fears in the heat of the moment.

In a sense, asking "What would they do?" becomes a safe place for you to retreat you when you are in an unfamiliar social situation.

Modeling

The notion of choosing a role model is not only socially proven, but also has roots in the psychology of learning.

It's known as *modeling*, and it is a method where people learn by observation and subsequent imitation alone, without instruction or explicit guidance. Patients and clients have been taught skills, behaviors, and habits just through modeling for decades — which means that finding your role model is more powerful than you probably imagined.

Modeling accounts for how we learned social cues, social norms, and even how to act at the dinner table. The landmark study on modeling and social learning was known as the Bobo Doll Experiment, conducted by Albert Bandura in 1961. In the experiment, children observed adults acting aggressively toward a Bobo doll — a doll which springs back upright after it is knocked down. One group of children observed the adults being rewarded after knocking the Bobo doll down, and subsequently began to model and imitate their aggressive behavior.

If we pay attention, we will begin to notice our tendency to emulate behavior. A younger sibling may see that his older sibling is rewarded for studying harder, so he will study harder. Conversely, the younger sibling my notice that his older sibling is only rewarded for athletic accomplishments, so he will shift his focus there.

Charisma role models are no different. We observe certain actions and traits, and we see our role models rewarded and lauded for them. We only want to emulate those ourselves so we can reap the rewards, as well.

However, just like the children in the Bobo doll experiment, we learn only what we are exposed to, for better or worse. We have a natural proclivity to pick up behavioral patterns from others, but how do we know which are positive and beneficial?

That's the importance of exposing yourself to charismatic people and actively thinking about how your role models would act. In fact, take it a step further, and however is practical for your lifestyle, surround yourself with social and charismatic people that you aspire to be like. If you feel supremely out of your comfort zone, that's even better, because it will push you to grow and evolve.

If you can't find it practical to physically surround yourself with more charismatic or social friends, even, then watch television shows, movies, interviews, and listen to podcasts that feature sharp, witty, charming people — perhaps even your role models. The more exposure, the better, because then it will start to be normalized in your mind and that's how habits form — when you don't have to consciously think about actions and behaviors.

Choosing a role model is important in every facet of life. We have career role models, health and fitness role models, and even fashion role models. Why shouldn't we have one for how we want to act with others?

Chapter 6. *Be* a Role Model

There's a saying that animals such as dogs and horses can sense how you feel, and if you feel fear or anxiety around them, it will cause them to be agitated, as well. However, if you project an air of calm and relaxation, these animals will feed off that energy in the same way and become docile themselves. This is likely where the phrase "they can smell the fear" came from.

People are actually the same way.

Imagine that you've just seen on the news that a tornado is headed your way. You immediately become alarmed and run to the grocery store to buy gallons of water and canned tomatoes. On your way back home, you run into your neighbor, and they don't seem concerned at all, despite having seen the same news. Your neighbor tells you that no one in the neighborhood is alarmed, and to just wear a scarf the following week.

Regardless of whether they are correct, their air of calm is undoubtedly going to make you relax. Whatever thoughts of destruction were running through your head are going to melt away, and you just might be able to get to the rest of your day in a normal fashion. A simple conversation and confirmation took you from DEFCON 1 to cooking burgers for lunch.

We take our cues on how to act from others, and charismatic people in particular act as role models because of how they can make people feel. A role model is someone whose behavior or thoughts are sought out and emulated by others.

Just like we want to be around those who are successful in business, we innately want to surround ourselves with charismatic people. There are many reasons why, but if we're honest with ourselves, it's because they inspire us and make us feel good about ourselves. Through them, we can see what's possible in the charismatic realm.

Just as we have our own role models as discussed in the previous chapter, you can task yourself with displaying charismatic behaviors so others can see *you* as a charismatic role model. This chapter is about how you can carry yourself in the face of adversity, difficulty, or everyday events in a way that other people will admire and take notice of.

There are a few specific traits you can begin to embody right away, and you will see that they all have common threads. You might be getting used to them yourself, but others will take notice.

Unflappable

Taking intimidation or awe out of the equation, we enjoy spending time with someone who inspires us to be better and makes us feel like everything will just be okay. That's the feeling we get when we are interacting with horses and dogs, and when our neighbor calms us down.

A uniquely charismatic trait is the ability to seem *unflappable* and like you've never had a bad day in your life, even if things aren't going your way. Of course, that's not true, so it's a matter of (1) perspective in seeing the big picture of life, and (2) becoming comfortable with that which is uncomfortable.

In the big picture perspective, tomorrow you probably won't remember or care about whatever ails you at the moment. Thus, by being affected, you are suffering needlessly and causing unnecessary stress in your life. Becoming comfortable with the uncomfortable and awkward parts of life is the understanding that not much good happens inside your comfort zone, and there are always proverbial vegetables we must eat in the meal of life.

They know it's an inevitable part of life and are able to brush it off as such. They have perspective on life and never allow themselves to be down for long. Awkward situations, different people, and uncomfortable situations do not faze them, and this is highly attractive to be around.

You can call it unflappability, strength, grit, willpower, or even discipline — whatever the case, it makes them a role model to aspire to, even if we don't realize it. Your ability to not let small stuff throw you off is part of your overall charisma. It's inspiring, gives others something to live up to, and drags up the moods of others around you. This is rooted in the realization that while you cannot control outcomes or guarantee certain conclusions, you can control how you act and react along the way. People instinctually like those who operate like lighthouses in any kind of foggy situation.

In social situations, unflappability makes people function like a home base. They have a very steadying presence and people are drawn to this. They feel that as long as they hang out with these people, they can weather an otherwise uncomfortable, tense, or awkward situation. When you see somebody retain their composure in any situation with anyone, it's inspiring. Charismatic people are even-keeled and always know what to do and what to say. It does not matter what is happening around them.

In essence, charismatic people appear bulletproof, and this has a very settling and attractive effect on the people they are with. They can diffuse the tension in a confrontation and make lemonade with grapes.

Charismatic people are anchors who refuse to be swept away by negative emotion.

Positivity

Of course, unflappability is closely related to positivity. Unflappability is about preventing your view of life from dipping below a certain number, where positivity is about creating a view of life that is as optimistic as possible given any set of circumstances.

Positivity begins with your inner monologue and the narrative you tell yourself about the world. Your inner monologue represents your deepest thoughts and desires without filter. This inevitably leaks out to affect your external world, and this can be good or bad. In other words, the results you get in life are caused by what you choose to believe in and how you choose to look at yourself. Your mindset influences your approach, which inevitably influences your actions. Negative people see life as a series of obligations and hassles.

For example, if your attitude is that you have to go to a meeting, then you have a problem on your hands. That phrasing is all about obligation and twisting your arm behind your back.

When your mindset reframes that situation as you get to go meet other people with the opportunity to make more money, what do you think the difference is? Here, you are dealing with a delightful privilege to benefit financially and socially. In the first scenario, you are dealing with a boring duty where you must go through the motions.

Something as simple as the word choice and phrasing you use can affect your mindset, which will accordingly produce different actions.

Pay attention to how you currently phrase things. You will be surprised as to how negative you are, and how much room there is for positivity. To be a role model, focus on working toward something and aspiring toward something. Work on seeing the good in anything and the side benefits, small as they might be.

If you're interviewing job candidates, you can view it as an obligation that will cause you to fall behind on your workload. Or you can see it as a privilege to select a great person to join your team and decrease your overall workload over time. Again, it is all about how you phrase the same set of facts.

You're not quitting a job, you're letting go of it to seek new opportunities for further growth.

When you focus on the positive, you focus on a sense of possibility, potential, and the greatness inside anything. The present might be unpleasant, but it's a necessary step to reach the overarching positivity and pleasure you want.

Use your vocabulary and phrasing to choose a sense of possibility, adventure, and what you have to gain in the immediate and long-term future. It's the ultimate glass-is-half-full mindset, and can make a true difference in your daily happiness.

Ultimately, it's your choice whether or not to be positive. You can proactively control how happy and positive you feel, or you can be passive and let other people and factors determine what happens to you.

Emotions

Charismatic people can be a bit of a puzzle. On one hand, you feel like you truly know them because of how comfortable they allow you to be. But on the other hand, you probably don't know much about them at all.

They've just acted in a way to make you comfortable so that you feel an instant bond with them. Charismatic people are socially powerful because they can draw people into their emotional world. Whatever they are feeling, they can make you feel. They also have the emotional intelligence to know what you are feeling to get on the same page as you.

To increase your charisma, you can't hide from your emotions and stay on a shallow level of interaction. Displaying your emotions is attractive, and people tend to wish they had the courage to do the same.

Charismatic people express their feelings in a very spontaneous way and can be said to wear their hearts on their sleeves.

There is a level of genuineness when people do not hold back on expressing what they are feeling inside. They don't filter what they want to express. There is a filter for tact, but there is still a very direct line from their thoughts to their words. People will feel like you are consistent and trustworthy because you express what you think.

Charismatic people can do this because they are unafraid to open themselves to judgment. It's empowering to see someone express themselves in such a way and creates an atmosphere of non-judgment for others to feel comfortable in and inhabit.

When you put yourself out there first and don't

appear to care, others will follow your emotional lead. People are grappling with their own level of emotional expression and intensity. We see people that we want to emulate, and an element that we feel is missing from our daily lives. They might even be a little jealous if you can express something that they always felt too scared or awkward to express themselves. This can become contagious, because the more you express your feelings, the more the people around you feel liberated regarding their own.

This is also true in terms of how vulnerable and open you allow yourself to be. Vulnerability is when you both willingly allow your weaknesses and flaws to show and accept them. It's a display of being comfortable with your own discomfort that inspires others to be more forthcoming.

Generosity

Become generous with your resources and your time, and give even though you may not get reciprocation. This builds an incredible goodwill that will have others scrambling to pay you back. This is something people will aspire to and admire you for.

The good news is that this doesn't have to involve

money, though it can. This doesn't have to involve tangible goods, though it can. You don't have give candy bars to everyone you meet.

You can focus on the giving the gift of your emotional support — for example, when you show genuine happiness at seeing someone or compliment someone. We live in such an alienated and busy culture that the simple act of genuinely smiling at somebody is quite rare on a day-to-day basis.

More often than not, people catch onto these gifts that you are bestowing upon them and will seek to reciprocate. If they do, that's just an added bonus to the charismatic presence that you are cultivating. The mindset of genuinely helping others even when it may not benefit you is invaluable.

Think of the last time you felt grateful to somebody. It was very hard for you to feel anger or animosity toward that person. You were probably in a place where it was easier for that person to persuade you. You were probably in a place where it was easier for that person to develop a strong personal connection with you.

Believe in the ultimate power of *karma* and stay

generous, knowing that even if there is no reciprocation from the person in question, there will be from someone or something else.

It may seem unnecessary to mention, but the true type of generosity you should target is where you have a complete lack of expectation. There's no ulterior motive. If there is a hint that you are only doing something for your personal gain, all of the goodwill vanishes and is replaced by defensive suspicion.

Generosity is ultimately charismatic because people feel that you're a good person with nothing to hide, and what they see is what they get. That makes people comfortable, and it doesn't hurt that you're always doing your best to help them.

Don't People-Please

Don't attempt to be friends with everyone, and don't try to make everyone happy. It's impossible, and you can't expect to achieve it because you'll always be paralyzed and unhappy.

If this is your personal philosophy, odds are that you aren't happy and comfortable enough with yourself to have the confidence that people will accept you for who you really are ... and you might never be truly happy, because you'll be constantly seeking validation and approval from others.

Unfortunately, this thinking highly affects how we relate and interact with each other. People feel that they have to say certain things and act a certain way to be accepted and appreciated.

The truth is that if you try to please everyone, you will become amazingly forgettable. Lukewarm. Blank. Just "nice." The lukewarm connections you make will rarely turn into real friendships, and instead remain stuck in acquaintance mode because people won't see the value in you. Certainly, they will not perceive you as someone to be emulated.

Charismatic people are never overly concerned with how they are perceived, or afraid of judgment, and this allows them to live with integrity to their true selves. You may be slightly polarizing, but the reality is in any type of social setting, you're bound to turn off certain people.

Even if you end up alienating 90% of the people you come across, why would you want to surround yourself with those who don't like your true self? What end does that serve? Why hang around others if they don't really like you, and you have to become a sanitized or false version of yourself to fit in with them?

When you stop the compulsion to people-please, you stop approaching others solely due to wanting to mitigate losses of favor. Many people approach others to not lose approval, instead of to win approval. The difference is that the former makes us act overly safe, and the latter lets us be ourselves. Show conviction in your beliefs and don't be afraid to disagree with others.

By being unapologetically you, you filter for your real friends. Real friends will enjoy you and accept you for who you are, not because of somebody you pretend to be. This is another facet of charisma that people wish they had the courage for.

Embracing the traits to be a role model for others makes you more charismatic as a matter of fact.

Chapter 7. Shine Your Spotlight

Regardless of whether you are drawn to politicians yourself, there is a reason they have so much appeal to literally millions of people.

If you look at what they say, they are elected because they make their constituencies feel heard and validated.

The politician might never have actually met of any his voters, but he makes it a point to focus on the needs of his voters and put their desires center-stage. In other words, he shines the spotlight on his voters in a way that makes it seem like he truly cares about them. Smartly, he realizes elections aren't so much about him, but about the changes people want in their lives.

Thus, in an ideal world, politicians make it a goal to step to the side and shine the spotlight on the needs of the people. Their purpose is to listen and only be a conduit for the people, and the people are much happier because it is all about them.

Though we may not realize it, this is exactly how we should act. The politicians who transparently approach citizens with a me-first attitude and emphasize what they are looking to get out of it usually go home as losers. Likewise, the people who approach others in a social setting with their own agenda, or simply wanting to preach or deliver a monologue, will usually go home as losers too.

To be more charismatic and captivating, devote your attention to other people and make the conversation all about them.

In other words, *shine your spotlight on them*; make them the center of attention or focus of a conversation. Think of it as preferring to throw parties for everyone else instead of celebrating your own birthday. Allow others to take center-stage, take praise, garner credit, and be the heroes in stories. In fact, make them the heroes of *your* stories. Be their greatest supporting actor and make it easy for them to be witty, make jokes, and tell good stories. If you know they had a funny week, prompt them to talk about it; if it seems like they want to engage in something, bring it up; if there is any doubt of where to go in the conversation, dig deeper into them; allow them to teach you something and make them feel like an expert.

By shining the spotlight on others, you impart a sense of importance and priority to them. Make it clear just how important others are to you, or how instrumental they are in making something happen. You are saying, "I am on your side, and want to hear how great you are."

A successful spotlight will result in someone just wanting you around more because you always bring up stories that make someone look like a stud. It also boosts the confidence and presence of the person who is basking in the spotlight. If they were unsure of how confident they should be with their new haircut or their new job, you've just made the decision for them: very! Bring people out of their shells and don't let them be bashful about positive or funny aspects of their lives.

It might seem understated, but when you are someone's supporting actor and you shine the spotlight onto them, the end effect is that you will make someone's day, or even their week. They may not remember what you did exactly, but they will remember walking away from interactions feeling good about themselves because you helped them present their best sides to others.

The effects of shining your spotlight on others and allowing people to speak about themselves are also scientifically proven, to an extent. Researchers at Harvard University discovered that the act of self-disclosure, talking about oneself, is intrinsically rewarding. They found that there was a large increase of neural activity in brain areas associated with pleasure and reward when people talked about or thought about themselves, even if no one was there to listen or observe.

At last, scientific evidence that we are all selfish and self-absorbed. We may be shy, introverted, or innate wallflowers, but that doesn't mean we still don't want to share information about ourselves and tell others about our thoughts and feelings. Indeed, we feel incomplete and unsatisfied when we walk away from a conversation where we were unable to share our opinions.

Surprisingly, shining the spotlight on others will also make you appear more confident, as it will become evident that you are capable of completely ignoring your own desire for the spotlight. It doesn't hurt that you'll appear humble and grounded, as well.

All you need to do is treat everyone like it's their birthday every day — make them feel special by letting them feel good about themselves. If they aren't giving you much to work with, use *rhetorical questions* to get them more involved and engaged.

In short, *when you talk, talk about them* — what they want, think, and enjoy.

Compliments

Another way to shine your spotlight on others is to give more compliments. When you're around people who constantly make you feel good, you want to be around them more often. The flip side is also true. If you come across people who are predictably negative and put you in a bad place, mentally and emotionally speaking, your tendency is to run away from them.

It is no surprise that people are naturally drawn to compliments. They're like psychological candy.

However, compliments are like pizza: even when it's bad, it's quite good. But there is a spectrum of worse and better ways to compliment people.

For instance, when I was a child, a teacher once complimented me on my smile. I remember this fact because I overheard the teacher saying the exact same thing to every child at various points of the school year. Thus, her compliment lost all significance to me. Unfortunately, a lot of people think that compliments are like candy. They believe the more candy they give out, the more other people will like them.

More is not always better. There is one key type of compliment I like to use over any others: things that people have made a conscious choice about.

You should compliment people on the things they can control like their clothing, fashion style, hairstyle, and living space. While these seem like just superficial, material things, they are also personal and impactful. People's personas and identities are reflected in the choices they make. By complimenting someone on something they've clearly chosen with purpose, you acknowledge and validate the statement they have chosen to make about themselves.

These things reflect who they are and what they've done, whereas complimenting them on something they don't have control over, such as their eye color, doesn't. The person has actual control over the things I listed, and they've made a choice. They've chosen their personal fashion style, their hair, and the way they've decorated their house or flat. These things reflect a person's tastes and values.

Choose things that they've obviously put some thought into. This might include a bright shirt, a distinctive handbag, an unusual piece of art, or a vintage car. These are things that are out of the ordinary, uncommon, and that reflect a deliberate deviation from the norm. What makes these compliments effective is that these kinds of personal statements are what make the person feel unique.

Other things you can compliment people about are their manners, the way they phrase certain ideas, their opinions, their worldview, and their perspective.

Now contrast complimenting choices people have consciously made versus complimenting one of their physical features, like their eyes or smile. It's nice, but it doesn't validate them as much because it's just something they were born with. You've also probably heard that compliment dozens of times in your own life, so it begins to lose impact very quickly. You could conceivably give that same compliment to 50 people that very day. There's no ownership over it.

It is the equivalent of saying, "You're so tall. It's very impressive!"

React

A proper reaction lets people know that you are listening and caring.

For instance, if you just heard a story about winning the lottery, what do you suppose the proper reaction might be? This can typically be split into three portions.

Verbally: words of congratulations, elation, excitement, joy.

Non-verbally: high-five, clutching your hands, jumping up and down.

Facial expression: smile, laughter, aroused (big) eyes.

These three aspects work together to form a complete reaction to a simple story about winning the lottery. They make it absolutely certain that you have heard what they have said, taken it in, and been impacted by it. You need to react to people's words with *importance*.

Reactions are the ultimate tool for validation because you are visibly being affected and acknowledging people. Even something as small as a nod can have a large impact on people. You cannot be a blank wall and take it all in with no emotional feedback whatsoever. Nothing about that communicates the fact what they are saying is important to you, and there's absolutely no emotional engagement.

People tend to edit themselves when they converse. Whenever they strike up a conversation, they are actually quite selective regarding the topics that they choose to dwell on. They're not brought up or allowed to continue without reason — these topics make people care.

If you just sit there and nod along like a robot, your interest not going to register with them. They'll probably think you are bored and disinterested — the opposite of making them feel important. The facial expressions, reactions, and gestures that you think are conveying a message likely are not.

The answer is to react with importance by following them emotionally. In other words, you are showing that you care so much about what they've said that you are emotionally affected. It sounds like a tall task, but it's much easier than you think. All you have to do is ask yourself what the primary emotion is that someone is trying to convey with their current set of statements.

Winning the lottery: joy.

Being cut off in traffic: annoyance, anger.

Going to a baseball game: excitement, happiness.

Then, after you determine the primary emotion someone is trying to convey, show it to them as they are conveying it. When you notice that they are getting heated at certain points in the story, get heated with them. Follow them on the emotional journey they are sharing — every story has a purpose and point, and it's almost always about how they were made to feel. This sends them a clear and unmistakable emotional signal that their feelings matter.

Show it to them with the aforementioned three portions of a full reaction: your words, your body language, and your facial expressions. Use all the tools at your disposal and make sure they are consistent and strong.

Imagine how great it feels when you arrive at your home and your dog greets you at your door. They're wagging their tail so intensely that it looks like it is going to fly off. This reaction drives home the point that you truly matter to them — you are special, and you are their world! While you don't need to exaggerate like a golden retriever, you should react in such a way that it is unmistakable and *not* subtle.

Validation is the recognition of someone's feelings as important and accepted. Let others know that you are validating their wants, thoughts, and emotions in a visible manner. It's the equivalent of saying, "Yes, he's terrible" when someone wants to rant and rave over their cruel supervisor.

Get into the habit of shining your spotlight onto other people and watch as they rise to the challenge. The less you focus on yourself, the more charismatic you will become.

Chapter 8. Goal Alignment

Goal alignment doesn't seem to be a term which fits into the cause of charisma, but it's actually extremely important because the goal you set for yourself influences all of your actions.

For instance, if your goal for the current year is to maximize your income through whatever means possible, you are going to work more, apply for more jobs, and generally have very little free time because you are pursuing your goal. You will probably fill your weekends with additional work and exploration of new projects that could lead to new sources of revenue.

By contrast, if your goal is to enjoy life more and live by the credo of *carpe diem*, then you are probably going to work as little as possible, perhaps even quit your job, and utilize your weekends to the max. You will likely spend as little time as possible at home, and always be trying to meet new people.

Socially, we can also see goals influencing our actions. When we walk into a job interview, our goal is to make a good impression, and thus all of our stories involve us acting as a hero or savior. Everything will have a positive slant, and we will glaze over our flaws or spin them into strengths somehow. We have answers prepared, and we are waiting for the interviewer to dictate the direction because it's all about what they want to ask.

Some of us carry this same goal of making a good impression into our regular conversations, and it results in exactly what happens in a job interview — except your conversation partner isn't an interviewer and isn't particularly interested in hearing about how great you are. That's why the notion of goal alignment can be so important — if you're approaching others with the incorrect goal, or a goal that doesn't make sense for the context, you can kiss your chances of charisma goodbye.

As you've read, in the social conversation context, having a goal of impressing the other person simply won't play well. You're not interviewing for anything, and if you continually try to talk yourself up, you'll come off as a self-absorbed blowhard. We all know people who forget that they aren't in a job interview — it becomes clear that they are stroking their own ego and bragging for their own benefit.

So what are some goals to *not* have in social conversation?

1. Impressing others and building yourself up.
2. Being charismatic and charming.
3. Being witty and funny.

Basically, everything that you thought you should be focusing on. But that's where the realignment becomes important. You've read what happens when you focus on impressing others.

When you focus on being charismatic, well, what does that even mean? You will likely be trying to captivate others with stories and engage them on shallow topics. And when you focus on being funny, you'll be taking every opportunity to crack jokes, even when they aren't funny. Both of these things will happen when you have a goal in mind, and these goals just happen to be detrimental to actually being charming and engaging. When you try to achieve these positive things, you will become artificial, forced, and just plain weird — like having a fake smile plastered on your face because you think it will move you toward your goal.

So what should we be realigning our goals to?

Self-Amusement and Entertainment

Self-amusement is geared toward you, and entertainment is geared toward other people.

This simply means one of your overarching goals with conversation and social interaction should be to (1) make it fun for yourself, and (2) make it fun for other people. Put another way, your goal when you speak to other people in a social setting should be to engage them and make it *not boring* for them and yourself. It might sound like a tall task, but this is an easier goal because there are literally infinite ways to accomplish it.

When you focus on amusing *yourself*, suddenly many filters are removed because you just want to ask or comment on what interests you. Likewise, when you focus on entertaining others, you're less inclined to stay on surface level small talk and engage on topics that are personal and varied.

Boring is death. You might have other goals in mind, but if you just provide an interaction that people are entertained by, it will be mutually enjoyable and anything else you want from it will flow naturally. If you want to make more sales or connect in a business context, people are going to be more willing to do so if they enjoy interacting with you.

This operates on the concept of classical conditioning, which is the notion that we subconsciously want people around who make us feel engaged, happy, and positive. You could even call that an alternate definition of charisma.

Many people drift from interaction to interaction without a goal or purpose, and are content to be unmemorable. Indeed, cultivating an air of self-amusement and entertainment can sometimes happen organically, but there are a few mindsets you can borrow to simply have more fun and less boring conversations. It would be nice if we could just wait for a mutually interesting topic to arise, but that's an attitude that is passive and puts you at the mercy of Lady Luck or other people making the effort. Instead, be proactive and manufacture the type of interaction you want by making the first move.

If you're in a boring conversation, you're at least 50% responsible. You have the power to control a conversation and make it as entertaining or probing as you want, so seize the reins and don't rely on others to entertain you. Embody the mindset that you possess the power to change your circumstances.

First, understand that everyone possesses a quirky and fun side.

They may not show it readily, or they may hide it under a professional façade, but what you see is not always what you get. For example, many people say they feel constrained at the workplace because they feel the need to be overly appropriate with their coworkers, but their coworkers are people too, and they have friends who act in silly ways. And yet, people tend to act in a freer and more unfiltered manner with anyone besides their coworkers. Point being, you may need to dig a little bit and find their quirky and fun sides, because for any number of reasons, they are keeping it subtle or held back.

To be entertaining (to others) and amusing (to yourself), it's your duty to dig below the surface and find what makes people beautifully abnormal or noteworthy. These are the personal differences that give us our identities, and more importantly, provide fodder for fun and playful conversation material.

Do you feel differently about coffee than Johnny? Why does he hate it and refuse to drink it under any circumstances?

Does someone comb their hair in a particular way? When did they start to do that? What's the story behind it, and why does it differ from your method?

Dig into people and their differences and share your own unconventional methods or views on a subject. This strays from the norm, and will make people react in ways that break their scripts and templates. In other words, a conversation they haven't encountered before, and one that isn't boring.

Go out on a limb, take a stance, and show conviction. It will also encourage them to share their own unique views on subjects, and suddenly you're in a real, substantive, and entertaining conversation.

When you encourage unusual and personal takes on a subject, you're being emotionally open with each other. Instead of walling off each other and condemning each other as unusual, this opens an opportunity for bonding. "You know what? We're not so different, you and I. I have that side to me too!"

The way people actually connect with others and enjoy their company is because of their idiosyncrasies. You don't become friends with someone because they meet your ideals or standards. You just find each other amusing and entertaining, and that's the entire basis of friendship at the outset. You make each other laugh, think, or engage. You have fun in their presence, and they have fun in yours.

Self-amusement begins with viewing others as opportunities to joke around. Develop the mindset of interacting with people and things in your daily life just to see what happens when you *poke* them, and it will serve you well in conversations.

Work on not filtering your thoughts as much. See what reactions you can provoke. Ask ridiculous hypotheticals. Seek to find the humor in any situation. Ask what hilarious situations something you see reminds you of. Compare an innocent bystander to a Disney character. Answer questions with movie references. Think out loud.

The common theme is you are the one initiating it. You can't rely on others to do the work for you, nor expect to be entertained by others like a sultan.

Don't be afraid to "go there" and jump into so-called taboo topics, because 99.99% of the time, people are completely fine with topics that others would call offensive, improper, or rude. The other .01% of the time, the topic is fine, but the timing or context is less than ideal.

Taboo topics are often more personal in nature, so in addition to creating an interesting line of conversation, you've just made it infinitely more personal and deep.

Most people are busy trying to be safe and stay polite. That approach is actually yawn-inducing and boring, and probably reflects their approach in other aspects of life. They're filtering themselves to a fault and not showing their true selves. If you act like everyone else, don't expect to make an impression.

Build Trust and Comfort

Another goal to focus on is to build trust, rapport, and comfort. Make people feel at ease in your presence, like they can open up and let their guards down. You can easily see why this might be important in cultivating charisma.

There are a few ways to be perceived as trustworthy. First, and perhaps most obviously, tell the truth, or make it appear that you value the truth. If you're going to build and project trust, it's important to be precise and exact with facts and numbers. We have a tendency to round up, editorialize, spin information, or omit facts that make us look worse.

This is all fine until someone finds out you weren't being completely truthful, and then the carefully constructed image you've created for yourself comes tumbling down immediately. Commit to telling the exact and precise truth and then dealing with it head-on, instead of hoping that it won't come up and dealing with the messy aftermath. If you are direct, people are usually more forgiving than you think, and they will feel that they can indeed trust you and let their guards down around you.

In a social setting, there is no expectation of perfection, but in the face of inevitable mistakes or errors, you must at least come clean. Hold yourself and others accountable, and don't blame others or deflect responsibility. This will give the appearance that all you care about is yourself, which is not a trait that begets trust.

This is also related to appearing transparent, or the appearance that you have nothing to hide, have no ulterior motives, and are exactly what you appear to be.

It might sound like you should appear positive and chipper with anyone you meet, but that's also not true. You have to have an element of genuineness so you don't appear fake, and show sincere reactions. If something is negative, you can talk about the negativity, and that will make you appear more objective and reliable. It shows that you are making judgments off of what you see, and that you aren't biased or making judgments based on preconceptions.

Perhaps counterintuitively, expressing your opinion — even if it is negative — can make you appear more trustworthy. A 2013 study from the University of South Carolina showed that people who voiced strong moral stances (positive and negative) were seen as more trustworthy, presumably because their ability to openly criticize was viewed as highly related to the existence of similar standards for themselves.

As long as you can do this in a manner which isn't hypocritical, preachy, or constantly unsolicited and abrasive, voicing your opinion is a trustworthy trait.

Finally, in the quest of building trust and comfort, try not to talk about others behind their backs — because the people you rant and rave to never know whether you'll be doing the same thing to them. There is value in discovering a shared hatred of someone, but the risk is often far greater than the reward of ranting together. When you refuse to talk about someone behind their back, or simply demur and remain mostly quiet, you'll appear to be more loyal and show an awareness of what is right and wrong. Again, it's this appearance of structure and standards that will make people feel safe around you. When you can create a safe space for people to inhabit, they'll lower their guards — after all, it's work to maintain them.

Overall, make people feel *good*. Make people feel good about themselves and about interacting with you. Set an overarching goal of having them walk away from an interaction with you feeling *good*.

Charismatic people are like supporting actors in many ways. They don't worry about their own glory or pride, and have no problem letting other people shine. They listen well, they validate people's emotions, and they often put their own needs to the side. They are the supporting actor in a two-person conversation, and they protect their lead actor.

They never address other people's errors. They do not judge. They know that everyone is fighting their own battle on some level, and they let sleeping dogs lie.

On a subconscious level, this draws even more people to them because there's no judgment. There is only acceptance and support. This is quite a departure from the goals we had articulated at the beginning of this chapter.

Chapter 9. Speak Their Language

Our caveman ancestors lived very different lives.

Instead of phones, they had rocks, and instead of McDonald's, they had to hunt their meals daily. Most of their lives were focused not on finding careers that they enjoyed, but on not being picked off by a wandering predator or succumbing to some type of sickness.

One of the most important evolutionary adaptations we made was to highly favor the familiar, and by extension, people who were similar to us (Nolan, 2013, and Gallup, 2010). This adaptation functioned in a very simple way: We tended to stay alive more frequently when we stayed close to humanoid shapes and shadows, as opposed to large feline shapes and shadows. We also tended to die less often when we ate berries and fruits that were familiar versus that which was foreign and a mystery.

Now that the only jungles most of us live in are of the concrete nature, survival is not usually the concern of preferring similarity and familiarity.

Similarity and familiarity were huge evolutionary advantages that still play a role in the decisions we make today. For instance, if you came across someone whom you discovered was a long-lost relative, you're likely going to instantly view them differently. You'll view them as more similar, more familiar, and with that, you will assign them a host of positive traits and adjectives.

The first assumption is that they are on your level status-wise, however you define the word. This is a powerful psychological component in being interested and curious in what someone has to say. If you feel that someone is the same status as you, or even slightly higher, you're simply going to want to make a good impression on them and connect more. This bodes well for any conversation.

The second assumption is that you are both privy to exclusive knowledge and experiences. The two of you inhabit a world that no one else knows about, so a strong bond is immediately created on the basis of sharing that specialized knowledge or experience. And just as with the first assumption, there is a psychological effect that is created that makes opening up and connecting all the easier.

The third and final assumption is that besides status, you are simply similar to them as a whole. People like people who are like themselves — it's a simple fact. People will also seek out others like themselves, be more likely to help others like themselves, and seek to integrate them into their friend circles. Don't we bond immediately with people from our same hometown or school?

These ancient instincts still hold fast, and we can take advantage of them when cultivating our sense of charisma. The underlying message in this chapter is to speak people's language. There are ways you can manufacture feelings of similarity and familiarity, and subsequently gain access to their inner circles.

Mirroring

Mirroring is the act of emulating elements of

people's exterior presentation — that is, everything you can see and hear of a person.

An earlier chapter implored you to mentally mirror a role model to better prepare for interaction, but this chapter is about mirroring the person right across from you and literally appearing to be more similar to them.

Get on someone's level and speak how they speak, act how they act, and use the same phrases they do — and you will instantly be more charismatic.

If you can reflect some of these elements subtly, it's inevitable that others will start relating with you more positively and openly. It's like you are their next-door neighbor from their tiny town in Russia — speak some Russian, throw in some local slang, use Russian mannerisms, and you're practically family.

When you can reflect these elements, others will start relating with you more positively. They feel that you get them. They feel that you understand them. When they see somebody that acts differently from them or is just unfamiliar, they feel that deep down this person simply does not get them because they are on a completely different wavelength. After all, throughout most of history, you were a threat. If you were a member of a northern army and you saw the uniform of a southern army member, disliking unfamiliarity could literally save your life. The way we act often reflects the way we think.

On the other hand, if you conduct yourself in such a way that you talk like them or you have used the same tone of voice and mannerisms, it is easier for them to relate to you because they feel that you are familiar enough to include in their comfort zone.

You are predictable in a good way. They will feel like they know how you think and how you will act and react. It will be easier for them to find you credible. Once people find you credible, then you're only a hop, skip, and a jump away from them trusting you.

What exactly do you mirror from others?

As I mentioned earlier, you can mirror their words, their tone of voice, and their mannerisms. Keep in mind that mirroring is not just about reflecting them on a wholesale basis. Instead, it is all about communicating to them that you share similar values and have the potential to connect intimately.

You can mirror physical signals, gestures, tics, and mannerisms. For example, if you notice that someone uses a lot of gestures when talking, you should do the same. Similarly, if you notice that someone's body language involves a lot of leaning and crossing of arms, you should do the same.

You can mirror their verbal expressions and expressiveness — tone of voice, inflection, word choice, slang and vocabulary, emotional intonation, and excitement and energy.

For example, if you notice that someone continually uses certain words and terms that you might use something else for, talk to them in their language. Similarly, if you notice that someone is excited and pumped about something, you should elevate your energy level so they don't feel that you are just bringing them down. Speed and volume matching is easy to do, and much less obvious than physical mirroring.

Subtlety is key.

If you are blatant or obvious in the way you mirror people you are talking to, you will end up repulsing them because it seems like you are mocking them. Instantly, instead of appearing similar and familiar, you might look like you have ulterior motives.

Though we're talking about doing this consciously, mirroring is something that occurs subconsciously when we are engaged with someone. This means it's something you can actually test. If you're speaking face to face with someone, you can subtly scratch your nose with the side of your finger, adjust your glasses, or make a particular gesture and see if it is mirrored. You'll be able to see how engrossed people are in *you*.

It's been recently discovered that mirroring works on a deeper level than just rapport-building.

Humans possess mirror neurons, which were discovered by Italian scientists working with macaque monkeys. When one of the researchers reached for his lunch, he noticed the brain activity of observing monkeys was as if the monkeys themselves were reaching for food. In other words, because the monkeys had seen an act, their brains also *felt* the act. Their brains were virtually identical when observing versus carrying out a physical act, and the brain cells involved were called mirror neurons, for obvious reasons.

In human beings, various studies (Kohn, 2010, among others) discovered that mirror neurons were not only about observing actions, but also about observing feelings and emotion. Whatever we see in other people, our brains also feel. It's essentially neurological sympathy that lets us relate to people better, walk in their shoes, and connect on an emotional level.

In a 2008 study, subjects who were told to use mirroring and mimicking of others reached better outcomes in simulated negotiations. In a 2010 study, it was discovered that when you observe someone mirroring your behavior, there is brain activity in the areas that process pleasure and rewards. Clearly there is something comforting and positive about mirroring others, so make it a habit to just copy what you see — that's where it starts.

Analogies

Another way to instantly get on people's level and speak their language is to become an expert at using analogies.

A metaphor is typically a figure of speech that makes a comparison, but I would encourage you to use a metaphor as a tool to be more relatable.

For instance, you might be trying to explain a technical concept, but you could compare it to a baseball batter getting a hit. You can use analogies to simplify and contextualize.

For instance, you might be trying to explain something simple, yet totally foreign, like how you feel about marriage. You can also use analogies to make people understand your point in a way that they relate to.

Realize that people don't always understand you, your subject matter, or your feelings. Thus, get into the habit of using analogies and metaphors more frequently to put things in terms others can understand.

This can be as simple as saying, "You know, it's like ..." or "It's just like X, minus Y ..." Provide meaning and significance for the listener so they can understand your emotions better. Analogies aren't just a throwaway comment at the end — put them in a prominent position and discuss within the framework of the analogy or metaphor for even better understanding. Staying within the analogy is the equivalent of physically mirroring someone's posture.

Instead of occupying the same physical appearance, you are occupying the same mental context, which is significantly deeper. Overall, analogies are an easy way to tailor and personalize your message and emotions to different people.

<u>Speak Their Language</u>

Speak their language. Use their terms. Take yourself into their verbal comfort zone and let them feel like they're at home.

You have to remember that everybody comes from different backgrounds. We all grew up in vastly different contexts, and that context informs both our perspective and our verbal comfort zone. If you want to become a truly effective conversationalist, you need to quickly figure out what this context is for others. It doesn't necessarily have to do with what you see, but rather, it can be about how people choose to *view* themselves.

An illustration might help a bit: Let's imagine that

you are speaking to someone with a thick British accent.

Will they be more comfortable with someone who (1) also has a British accent and uses the words "lift," "loo," and "bloody" every other sentence, or someone who (2) doesn't know the significance of those words, or who has trouble understanding a British accent?

We all have comfort zones — that doesn't make us xenophobic or exclusive. It's just something that happens naturally as a result of our upbringing. Finding someone's comfort zone is similar to mirroring, except here you are speaking his or her language instead of just copying it.

Observe the vocabulary and vernacular someone uses. To use someone's vocabulary can make a huge difference in how they perceive you. You immediately set yourself aside from others and put yourself on someone else's level. If they don't have to translate the terms that they do for other people, it's a relief, to some degree.

This is a subtle piece of advice, because sometimes there just isn't that much proprietary vocabulary to latch onto and reflect back to them. If you can make it feel like they are talking to their childhood neighbor, that's a good thing. Their core is always what people are comfortable with.

With just a tiny bit of background research, you can discover people's contexts and comfort zones before you even talk to them. For example, you could ask your friends where someone was raised or what their favorite hobbies were. Armed thusly, you could sprinkle in phrases and vocabulary that are inherent to those locations or hobbies, and instantly break the ice and force them to see you on their level.

For example, if you learn that someone was raised in a rural village and their favorite hobby is skiing, you could use rural vocabulary when talking about livestock, and use an analogy or metaphor that involves ski lifts and slopes. You'll probably see their eyes light up with recognition of someone that they can relate to intimately.

As an example of how someone might internally view themselves, let's take a high-powered attorney who is making several million dollars a year as a law firm partner. But if they talk to you mostly about farming and life in the country and working with their hands, then that is the language they speak. The objective reality might be that this person is a true urban dweller, but their hearts and minds belong in the countryside. View them in the way that they prefer and speak that language.

But don't go overboard.

Unfortunately, we've all seen instances of this. It probably happens every time we see politicians speak on television. They awkwardly attempt to speak like the constituents they are addressing, often to hilarious results. Picture a 50-year old attorney addressing a 15-year old urban youth and using the type of slang they assume teenagers like to use. It's often cringe-worthy. You might also picture your own parents trying to keep up with acronyms, slang, and phrasing born of the Internet.

By speaking someone's language, it makes them feel like they can be 100% themselves around you. They don't have to put on a mask or show to gain your acceptance or understanding.

Chapter 10. Charisma No-Nos

At this point in the book, I've prescribed many things for you to establish habits around or pay more attention to.

While they are all important, and none can be said to take greater significance than the other, it's also important to avoid a host of the *charisma no-nos* you'll find in this chapter. Sometimes, it's just as important to avoid bad habits and repellant behaviors as it is to embody the positives.

People are more highly motivated by avoiding pain and displeasure than they are of seeking pleasure. That is to say it doesn't matter if you are amazingly charming otherwise — if you embody one or two of these repellant habits, people will avoid you like the plague and you will instantly become "that person" in your social circle or office.

Some of the charisma no-nos here are merely prescriptions for smoother interactions, while others will help you turn from someone people avoid into someone people seek out.

Just Let Go

I've described this phenomenon as being a full-fledged member of the Belief Police (BP).

You're part of the BP if:

1. You feel a strong need to be right.
2. You can't stand when people disagree or think differently from you.
3. Agreeing to disagree is unacceptable.
4. You become consumed by imposing your thoughts on others.

Sound familiar? A member of the BP may be normal and even charming, but if they come across something they don't like, or feel the need to correct, then all bets are off and you know what you will be talking about for the next 10 minutes.

You've got something to say, and you won't accept the fact that someone thinks differently, which in your perception is incorrect. Yes, we all have these compulsions from time to time, and sometimes they do matter. But it's also important to carefully choose your battles and not wield your BP badge frequently, otherwise people will treat you like the real life Gestapo: by avoiding you as much as possible.

You can correct people, and you can assert your opinion. But there are ways of doing that in a less abrasive way than outright telling people they are wrong, or pedantically correcting something that doesn't matter just to steal someone's thunder. You may even be correct, but that doesn't matter in the context of cultivating charisma.

The worst case scenario what will usually happen: defensiveness. Defensiveness is a gut reaction most of us have to being told we are wrong — which is tantamount to being verbally attacked. We shut down, and we start lashing back in an emotional manner. It's the mental equivalent of being attacked with a baseball bat: We fall back on our lizard brain (the fight or flight response) and are prepared for battle. Then it becomes an adversarial showoff that is focused on winning and defending because you've offended someone.

Not quite what you'd have in mind for a charming afternoon over a cup of tea. The lesson here is to relinquish your membership in the BP *and let people think different thoughts from you*. There's nothing at risk besides your pride and ego, which admittedly can feel enormous, at times.

In summation: Don't assume you're right, other people will agree with you, or nitpick irrelevant things.

Even Keel

Keep an even keel. The essential meaning is to control and regulate your emotions, at least on the outside.

Not that you shouldn't express your emotions freely and show your vulnerability, but you should probably cap them at a certain level of intensity for those outside your inner circle. The reason has to do with simple predictability.

When people feel that they know what to expect from you on the emotional spectrum, that's comforting. They know it can't get worse than a certain level. However, when you express negative emotion with great intensity in front of other people, they are going to become extremely uncomfortable, because they've just lost that sense of predictability surrounding you. They have no idea what you're capable of on the negative side of the spectrum.

For instance, if you make fun of someone's weight and they laugh it off, that's comforting, because it's predictable and you know this person is relatively comfortable with their weight. However, if you make fun of someone's weight and they shriek at you and start sobbing, then you might feel scared because you had no idea that was going to happen, and you don't know them as well as you thought.

Additionally, you'll feel like you have to walk on eggshells for the foreseeable future because you clearly have no idea what can set them off, or just how emotionally volatile they are. You don't want to be someone they take their misery out on when they are feeling bad. That's why keeping an even keel is so important — you become predictable in the sense that people aren't scared of what you might be capable of.

There are ways of managing those dark thoughts

and emotions that make you appear even-keeled and stable. Whether it's through meditation, aggressive physical activity, or just silent stewing, these are all better than lashing out or breaking down. Keeping control will show strength and is a highly admirable trait that people will notice. Of course, practicing emotional regulation also helps you in other areas of your life because it teaches you to move on and not dwell on the negative.

Relax

In other words, don't take everything so seriously.

There are usually at least two ways to interpret and react to a statement such as, "I can't believe the coffee is so good!"

First, there is a serious way, which focuses on facts and the information at face value. This is likely what you feel when you're stuck in small-talk mode. You can't break out of the conversation about the coffee because you feel like you have to respond literally and stay within the topic. "Yes, it's great, isn't it?"

The second way is to interpret it in a non-serious manner. This is where you will focus on being playful and try to find the humor or non sequitur in everything. Play more, amuse yourself, and poke around random topics. Say something like, "This coffee is terrible" with a straight face. Instead of reacting in a way that takes you down a path of boredom, react in a way where you are verbally jousting in an enjoyable manner.

Relaxing and not taking things so seriously has many dimensions. It also means curbing your cursing, complaining, negativity, judging, and gossiping. These habits are acceptable in moderation, but it makes you look petty and easily disturbed when you can't let go and appear fixated. Appearing relaxed has the same effect as the previous no-no of being even-keeled. The more relaxed you appear, the more people will grow comfortable around you. No one wants to spend time with someone that either goes on frequent tirades, or they feel they have to defend themselves to. It's the opposite feeling we want with a friend, because with a close friend, we feel uninhibited and unfiltered. If you can't confidently say what you want around a friend, then what are they for? You can't possibly consider them a *close* friend.

Sharing Too Much/Little

When you think about sharing information, it's a

bit like the conundrum Goldilocks faced.

You can't share too *much*, because people aren't interested in your dirty laundry, nor are they interested in the mundanities of your life. You can't share too *little*, because people won't have anything to respond to and you'll be contributing essentially nothing to the conversation.

Sharing too much: "So there we were, Friday night. Well, actually, it was Saturday morning because it was so late, but you know what I mean. Then Taylor comes over, and we get down to serious business. Which was great because my parents weren't home; they're in the Bahamas right now. I'm so jealous. I've always wanted to go. They even took a first-class flight to get there. Wow. Anyway, Taylor came over …"

This is far too much detail, and this person, while they are verbose and say a lot, doesn't actually *say or communicate* anything. They backtrack frequently, focus on small details that are irrelevant, and completely lose the overall narrative of the story, which presumably has something to do with Taylor on a Friday night. This is a textbook example of someone finding their way as they speak, essentially thinking out loud.

This is torturous for the listener, and most will soon tune out.

On the flip side, here is sharing too little: "Friday was fun. Taylor came over."

There is far too little detail for anyone to react to, and it's like you're prying teeth out of their mouth to get an answer. To get any detail, I would have to ask at least three to four questions, and that's tiring and annoying. Most people aren't going to hang in that long, and again, they will tune out soon. Not sharing personal information is one of the greatest downfalls of conversation, and thus, charisma.

You might be frustrated when other people do this to you, but you might not realize you are guilty of it too! It's doubly frustrating because it makes the recipient of the barren answer have to carry the burden of the conversational work. In essence, you are making is hard for people to talk to you, and when something turns difficult, they will stop doing it.

Thus, we have to ride a fine line between not sharing enough, and conversely, sharing too much information. Err on the side of sharing more, but make sure what you are sharing is actually a different, distinct piece of information, rather than backtracking or irrelevant. Then just stop talking. Shoot for five distinct details or pieces of information, and don't shy away from divulging personal information or opinions and stances. Each distinct detail should be able to stand on its own and lead down a separate path of discussion.

If you've done your job, you won't be met with an awkward silence which indicates confusion about where to go conversationally.

Be Aware

Specifically, be aware of when people have stopped listening, stopped paying attention, or stopped carrying in a conversation.

This is one of the biggest repellant habits to correct, and it doesn't take much thought to do so.

If someone has stopped replying to you with complete sentences and has reverted to one-word answers, they are on their way out.

If someone keeps looking around the room and searching for more options, they have a foot out the door.

If you don't follow up on something they bring up once, that might be fine, but if they swing back to that topic and you don't follow up on it, they will want to turn around immediately. People say things for a reason.

If you are talking about yourself most of the time, they will grow tired of smiling and nodding.

If you constantly interrupt and don't let people finish their thoughts, or steal their thunder and turn it back to yourself, people will be extremely annoyed.

If you are unable to let go of your own thoughts and either (1) pay little attention to people, or (2) don't cede the air to others, people will become frustrated.

Finally, if you feel like you have to constantly prod people with, "Right?" or "You know?" then it's probably because they are staying quiet in an attempt to make you feel bored and unengaged enough to wander off.

In summation: Do none of these things, or at least be aware of them.

Charisma no-nos are plentiful, and as you can see, some are grave and some are trivial, but they all contribute to a cumulative effect. Once people decide you possess one no-no too many, they simply will not want to bother with you anymore, and you know what that means for you!

Chapter 11. Quickness and Violations

Much of what has been presented in this book thus far may not be surprising to you. For some, they might be helpful reminders, and for others, they might be mere extensions of what you already know.

Many of the tips might be intuitive, and even obvious, in hindsight. There are many aspects of human interaction that we pick up just from being a functioning member of society, like basic manners or tucking in your shirt when you want to appear more tidy and clean. It's not until they are pointed out that they become clear, but nonetheless, the art of being charming isn't necessarily rocket science.

Thus, in this chapter, I want to take the

opportunity to present two in-depth studies about what truly makes people likable and charismatic. These might not be so obvious in hindsight, and they have ben proven and confirmed with scientific rigor.

Quicker is Better

The first study is titled *Quick Thinkers Are Smooth Talkers: Mental Speed Facilitates Charisma* and was conducted by William Von Hippel and his associates in 2015. As you might gather from the name, their general discovery was that speed of thought and dialogue was more highly related to people's ratings of charisma than many other traits, including being correct or accurate.

The researchers asked test participants to rate how quick-witted, funny, or charismatic their friends were depending on how they performed on a series of tests. Friends of the participants were also present and observing the tests.

In the first test, participants were asked to answer trivia questions given out in rapid succession. Afterwards, the participants' friends were asked to rate their friends who actually took the tests.

Conventionally, you would think that the friends of the participants would rate their friend as more charismatic, quick-witted, or funny depending on how frequently they answered correctly in the first test. That was not the case whatsoever. It turns out charisma wasn't related to accuracy, or even the appearance of intelligence.

What mattered most was how quickly the participants answered — the speed with which they took action.

Keeping in mind the parameters of the experiment didn't specify a right answer, the friends of the participants didn't necessarily care whether the participant performed the task correctly. All they based their decisions on was how quickly they answered.

The researchers concluded people tend to have a more favorable impression of you depending on how quickly you speak or take a position. It doesn't really matter whether you are correct in your position. People tend to have a natural attraction to others who "think on their feet," and the accuracy of your statements doesn't matter as much as how quick and sharp you seem to other people. Clearly, speed is associated with intelligence and social acumen.

So to appear more charismatic, it's clearly better to speak first and loudly, even if you have nothing to say, and even if you are speaking gibberish. Slow and silent, while it may not be seen as negative, clearly won't have the overwhelming positive effect that acting quickly will have.

At the outset, this seems absurd, because the study seems to suggest that talking out of your behind, as long as it is quick and confident, will make you more likable. Then again, is it actually so surprising?

When someone replies to a question or provides an opinion or stance quickly, we assume they are confident and knowledgeable — because only those types of people would move quickly. So, because we assume that people will only speak quickly if they have something valuable to say, if someone speaks quickly, we assume it's valuable. In other words, if X, then Y, where X is knowledge and confidence, and Y is speed.

The study confirms that we think if Y, then X, which is simply incorrect. However, we can use this knowledge to our advantage.

Speak first and speak quickly. You can always correct what you said. What's important is that you were able to say something quickly when prompted. When you're talking to people, make it your priority to respond in any way possible. Silences and lulls are your worst enemy. In many cases, the person probably won't care whether you have the right answer or not; they just want some type of answer or response.

If you're overly concerned with giving a correct, accurate, or even perfect response, your charisma quotient will drop if it's done slowly.

For instance, if you meet somebody at a party and they're talking about a problem they have at work, they don't expect you to actually solve their problem. They put it out there for the sake of conversation. If you respond to the information that they shared by digesting it slowly, turning it many times in your mind and cross-referencing it with your past experiences, it may take you a painfully long time to answer. By that time, the conversation has probably taken many different turns, or will be well on its way to ending.

A quick *anything* is better than a slow monologue. After all, isn't that what we see in movies and television shows — flowing banter that is quick like a ping-pong match? You might have to fight your mental programming to not speak in platitudes or speak just to make noise, but you should in pursuit of charisma.

Speak first, and you can always backtrack afterwards and correct yourself: "Let me rephrase that," or "Going back to what I said, I have a different approach."

You can also speak first, and think through your thoughts out loud, and find your way as you are speaking: "Well, see, that's an interesting point. What do I think about it? Good question. Here's what I think. It might be good, but it could also be bad because ..."

What's important is to maintain the momentum of the conversation. Keep that tempo, pace, and rhythm going by filling the silence and thinking quickly to be perceived as charismatic. Considering a large amount of social responses in a brief window of time is far less important than you'd think, and mental speed and alacrity is far more valued. Humans are emotional beings, and speed and confidence of presentation are always going to elicit a stronger emotional response than a well-thought-out answer.

An easy way to be quicker is to practice *free association*. Open any book and blindly put your finger on a page. What word did your finger point to? Now, quickly as possible, think of five words, things, people, places, concepts, or thoughts the word makes you think of. Without filtering. Then repeat the process with another word. The ability to pivot from topic to related topic is the backbone of flowing conversation. Your speed of thought will increase greatly, and you'll be a verbal ping pong master when you improve at free association.

The researcher Von Hippel perhaps summed it up best: "Although we expected mental speed to predict charisma, we thought that it would be less important than IQ. Instead, we found that how smart people were was less important than how quick they were."

Violations Are Funny

The second study is about exactly what we find funny and why. It turns out there is a science to what some might call crude humor — it functions on a principle called *benign moral violations,* which is something proposed in the 2010 research paper *Benign Violations: Making Immoral*

Behavior Funny by professor Peter McGraw at the University of Colorado - Boulder.

Humor is mostly seen as subjective, and we can see this to be partially true as humor does not tend to translate across cultural lines. For instance, there are no comedy movies that have consistently struck gold in international box offices because humor is rooted in language and contextual norms. However, action and adventure movies routinely break box office records because there's no cultural translation required for an explosion or flying car.

Thus, humor is unreliable, and you can't assume just because you find something funny other people will even smile.

According to McGraw, there is one approach to humor that is fairly universal and consistent. Regardless of who you're with, the culture you're in, or the social context you find yourself in, you can always draw on the power of the benign moral violation.

Researchers asked participants about hypothetical situations that breached a widely recognized social norm, such as farting in public or spilling a drink all over your supervisor. The researchers only asked two questions:

1. Was the behavior *immoral or wrong* to some degree?
2. Was it funny?

There was a very high correlation between the two — meaning the more immoral the behavior, the funnier it was rated. However, if the behavior was too immoral, then it quickly became unfunny. This is where the researchers coined the term "benign moral violation" — the act needs to be immoral, but in a way that appears harmless, distant, and has no negative repercussions. To be truly benign, the violation should be purely amusing, inoffensive, and psychologically distant, which means it doesn't appear real or tangible.

Other examples include:

1. Someone falling over and their pants coming off in the process.
2. A ball hitting someone in the crotch.
3. Making a gaffe when meeting someone famous or important.

See how these are a bit crass and *wrong*, but ultimately harmless because nothing is hurt besides people's sense of pride? Toilet humor is universal, and now we perhaps understand why!

Overall, this study tells us we shouldn't be too afraid of *going there* when talking to other people.

You may have come across the advice that you should stray from talking about religion, sex, and politics, but in some cases, if we find them as theoretical, hypothetical, and otherwise distant, what we say about them can come off as funny. It really all boils down to whether the moral violation involved in this story is benign or outrageous. If it's silly and outrageous, it's benign, and you've got a good chance of tackling tough topics. However, if it hits too close to home and becomes serious, then it's not benign and just becomes plain offensive.

What makes a violation funny is people are openly talking about something they have been trained not to — just a little bit over the line while not completely obliterating it. The tricky part is to know just how far you can push the envelope.

Without a proper sense of social calibration, it wouldn't be difficult to overdo things and focus so much on the shock value that you achieve the complete opposite effect. Instead of people finding you funny with an interesting sense of humor, they would instantly dismiss you as an overstepping ass.

Additionally, your moral violation can't be too benign, otherwise it will be run of the mill and boring. On the other hand, your moral violation can't be too great of a violation, otherwise people will be supremely uncomfortable and even emotionally affected. It's a quite a tightrope to walk. Unfortunately, if you don't practice this, it's too easy to make the wrong call.

Make people laugh with the violation, but remain comfortable because it's benign. If someone falls on their face in front of you, there will be initial shock and worry. But if you discover they tripped by stepping on a banana and they are 100% fine and unharmed, then you are going to find this situation funny because — hey, it is.

Closely related to this idea of the benign moral violation is the German concept of *schadenfreude*, which is defined as finding pleasure or amusement from someone else's suffering. It's only mean-spirited and in poor taste if we laugh when someone is truly hurt, but to laugh when someone has been violated in a benign way is very natural and widespread.

The underlying point is it's not negative to talk about negative things. You can bring up negative topics, moral violations or not, without turning your conversation sour.

The conclusions from these two studies may not be immediately obvious in hindsight, but they are certainly things we can incorporate into our interactions.

Chapter 12. Effective Listening

According to a recent statistic, most marriages in the United States break down not because of infidelity or money issues, but because of a failure to communicate and ineffective conflict resolution (YourTango, 2013).

This might seem obvious to some, but it underscores a few important facets of our relationships.

If you think people's abilities to engage in social conversation are bad, then people's abilities to engage in meaningful conversation that contains conflict are even worse.

People are flat-out bad at clear communication and effective listening. Even within the supposedly safe confines of marriage, people have issues with difficult conversations and the things that need to be said. People can't say what they want, and they can't or are unwilling to hear what others want. There is more to listening than sitting quietly and waiting for your turn to speak.

Communication issues arise when there is miscommunication, and if you can't accurately convey a feeling or hear what others are saying, they will be unavoidable.

People like to think they are being communicative, when in reality, they are doing the bare minimum to assuage their own feelings of guilt or obligation. Conversations that make people uncomfortable are often avoided, but most of them could be made far less painful if there was more effective listening.

As I mentioned, listening goes far beyond being present and waiting patiently for your turn to speak. Listening is synthesizing what someone tells you and dropping any pretense, responding to exactly what they said and nothing less. It requires dropping your own train of thought, because it is literally impossible to pay attention to your own thoughts while devoting your attention to someone else. You may recall this conundrum from one of the earlier chapters on being present and focused on others.

Truly effective listening is about shining the spotlight on the other person and reading them as completely as possible as to the kind of interaction they want to have.

This chapter is about becoming a great listener, which can go far beyond being engaging and charismatic. It just might salvage your friendships or relationships.

It's Not About You

The first step, which might begin to sound familiar, is to actually focus on the speaker. When you're listening, it means that your mouth is completely shut, and there is nothing coming out of your mouth besides an acknowledgment that you are focusing on them.

You might be dedicated to focusing on them, but they need to see it externally and receive feedback that you (1) are not simply waiting for your turn to speak with something on the tip of your tongue, and (2) you are actually acknowledging and digesting what is being told to you.

Many people like to pride themselves as good listeners based purely on the fact that they let people rant about their lives. The act of sitting silently does not make a good listener; it just means you are good at nodding and saying "Uh-huh …" At the end of it all, the only person who feels good about that interaction is the person who thinks they are listening well, because the speaker won't be getting any value from it.

Real listening focuses on the speaker. Clear your mind and create a blank slate. Show them *while* they are speaking with your gestures, nods, and verbal affirmations.

Instead of thinking about your trials and tribulations and what's happening in your life, wrap your mind instead around the life of somebody else. Wrap your mind around what's important to them and focus closely on the collection of ideas, emotions, and revelations coming from the speaker. This may seem easy, but it isn't, because we have the innate habit of thinking *me first*.

If someone comes to you with a story about how they were fired from their job, clear listening would be to completely ditch anything you wanted to say, resist the urge to speak up, and focus on them.

Here's a story a client related to me about resisting that urge.

> *My last breakup took a mental toll on me because I had invested so much into the relationship. Despite that investment, I knew it had to end at some point and just couldn't see it culminating in marriage.*
>
> *So I took the news to my best friend and really just wanted to unleash everything that was in my heart and head at that point. What transpired was incredibly frustrating. I would talk about the aspects of the relationship that weren't working for me and made me reconsider my entire life course.*
>
> *Then she started talking about how she did that with her husband, and then how her husband's family went on a trip to Israel that past summer. And then how that trip was horrible and led to some family discord. She stole my damn thunder.*
>
> *Normally, I'm a more than willing ear, but*

*this was a low moment for me, and she
failed to recognize that she needed to kick
her listening mode into gear. She flipped
the focus of the conversation from me to
her in a frustrating series of side thoughts
and thinking out loud.*

You can feel the frustration seeping out of his
statement. Listening isn't about you, no matter
how related it is, or how funny of a joke you can
make about it. It's about suppressing your urges
and relinquishing the center-stage to someone
else completely. Your job is to give them safe
emotional space where they can explore ideas, be
honest with feelings, and otherwise come up with
a sense of clarity.

You flush all these down the toilet when you talk
over them or switch the focus of the conversation
to yourself. It goes beyond stealing their thunder
and serves to make the other person feel
marginalized and unimportant.

More often than not, they're the ones who know
the answers regarding their problems, not you. So
it's really important to fight the urge to dominate
the conversation.

Listen With Intent

As I mentioned, effective listening isn't just quiet processing; it's acknowledging and taking words in, synthesizing them, and formulating specific feedback and follow-up. There's an intent behind it — you are listening for the purpose of helping the other person.

Effectuate your intent by always following up. A real follow-up question is when you put yourself in their shoes and try to understand the details they have to deal with. If you're talking to somebody who just lost his job, put yourself in that emotional state.

How would you feel if your home mortgage was due the next month and you lost your job? How would you feel if your kids came home and saw that their daddy didn't have a job anymore?

That's what your follow-up discussion should revolve around. The center must gravitate around what is important to the speaker.

A great conversation is a journey, not the destination. It's not a mad rush toward a fixed answer that doesn't change. Instead, it's really just about the process of the person letting their emotions out, picking through the details, and having another person be there to share the experience.

By listening with intent and always following up, you are helping them on their journey and acting as the catalyst. Most people's problems are easily solvable through their own actions, but they often need to arrive at that conclusion themselves. Focus on being curious and inquisitive, because that will help others elaborate and draw their own conclusions.

Another way to effectuate your intent of helping others is to create a sense of safety and non-judgment. If someone senses they will be subject to judgment, they simply won't share with you, and you will be unable to help them. This is, in a sense, one of the worst ways to listen, because judging actively makes it about your own thoughts. You're interjecting your opinion where it was not requested, nor welcome, and in doing so, you sever the lines of comfort.

Listening doesn't take an advanced degree, but it takes a lot of heart, empathy, and compassion.

Focus on the feelings and emotions that are in the background. These are the real reasons there is communication in the first place. It's not that a hat was stolen; it's the sense of loss of security, for example. There's often no logical explanation that will satisfy people in light of an emotional event. Even if the logical explanation is completely correct, it's a very dry, unfulfilling answer because people are suffering from emotional pain.

As such, whenever possible, name the emotions people are feeling or call them out. Naming emotions gives structure to what others are feeling and lets them understand their own reactions better. They won't feel like they are flailing as much.

"You seem devastated and unhappy because they left. Is that it?"

"I would be frustrated and in pain, if I was you."

When emotions are defined, they can start to formulate a response and reaction to it because suddenly, it's something familiar they have probably faced many times in their lives. Give them room to agree or disagree with what you've named, and they will dig deeper to elaborate to you, and consequently, themselves. You're helping them gain greater awareness over their emotional states, and though they might not realize it, they'll be glad for it.

As a final part of listening with intent, make it a goal to absorb absolutely all the information that is being conveyed and expressed. Be an information collector and try to catch the small hints people are trying to give you, if they don't want to say something directly. Again, this requires the utmost of attention on them, and a total abandonment of your own thoughts.

Reflecting

Reflecting, otherwise known as active listening, is one of the best tools for effective listening because it validates others. All you're really doing is summarizing what they've said or their feelings on the matter, but it shows to others you are truly attempting to understand them.

It will help people sort through their feelings and thoughts. As they attempt to explain their feelings to you, they will find themselves. For example, it can be as simple as saying, "So it sounds like you feel ..." The beauty is that once you grow comfortable with reflecting statements, it can feel almost robotic, because all you need to do is repeat the other person's words or sentiments. If you're correct, they will agree and elaborate further. If you happen to be incorrect, they will disagree and elaborate further. In either case, you are getting closer to the heart of the matter and mutual understanding.

Here are other validating, reflecting statements to make people elaborate and feel more heard:

1. What do you mean by [repeat the last phrase of their statement or story]?
2. In other words, [summarize their sentiment]?
3. You're telling me [summarize their sentiment]?
4. It sounds like you feel [make an assumption about their emotional statement]?
5. So [summary of sentiment]? Just that simple?

You can see how people would be prompted to respond to any of these questions. It will force them to reflect on their own thoughts and feelings and construct a narrative that logically includes both of them. Sometimes, that may be all they need to feel better about an experience that is troubling them.

When you reflect, you are getting to the heart of the matter and telling people that you hear them. You're not necessarily agreeing with them, but you are telling them their feelings are understandable and valid. Validation allows people to gain a sense of normalcy about their particular situation and lessen any negative feelings or the feeling that they shouldn't *feel*.

Never use the phrase, "I know exactly how you feel" unless you have been in that exact situation. It's simply a lie that isn't helpful to others — you don't have to agree with them; they just need to feel that they aren't crazy.

Effective listening embodies many of the traits of charisma we've covered, so it's no surprise it can have such a big impact.

Chapter 13. It's Not What You Say

In 2012, Harvard professor Amy Cuddy gave a TED talk about the concept of *power posing* and the subsequent effects on people's confidence.

What she found was holding what she called *The Superwoman Pose* (just as you might imagine it, standing stoically and powerfully with your legs spread and your hands on your hips, chin up like wind is blowing in your hair) for just two minutes is enough to raise your testosterone and lower cortisol levels, which has the cumulative affect of greater confidence and lower anxiety. Testosterone rose by as much as 19%, and cortisol fell by as much as 25%, and added with the self-perception of strength, power posing has made its way into popular media.

It was one of the first concrete pieces of evidence that sometimes, you can truly live by body over mind, and your body can exert certain control over your state of mind and thoughts. It's especially significant for our purposes because it means no matter how weak, tired, or un-charming you may feel, there are ways of unlocking the confident energy inside you to become more charismatic.

Sometimes it is indeed not what you say to someone, but how you appear — your body language, facial expressions, and everything non-verbal. If someone was cordial to you, but you still walked away with a feeling of, "That man just gave me a bad feeling," then it was due to something non-verbal you consciously or subconsciously observed.

This means there are two distinct benefits from being cognizant of your body language and optimizing it. First, according to Cuddy's study, you will literally change your brain chemistry with better posture and receive more positive feedback as a result. Second, you will prevent people from pre-judging your poor, unconfident, or even hostile body language and labeling you as a jerk before you say a word. Studies have estimated that approximately 55-93% of all communication is non-verbal, so it's fitting that I saved this for the last chapter.

Smiling

Smiling counts as body language because it doesn't make a sound. Therefore, it's something people can pre-judge your entire personality on!

Any time you talk about smiling, the first thing that comes up is the concept of the *Duchenne smile*. It was named for a French doctor who was one of the founders of modern neurology, and if you were to conduct any independent research on him, you might be amused to see the pictures of him that are most popular.

The reason is one of Duchenne's main thrusts was to study facial expressions and how they are related to emotions. Thus, many of the existing pictures of him are his contorted face trying to express different emotions. Of course, he was extremely interested in how smiles seemed to be universal and how they came about. He discovered all facial expressions are essentially muscle contractions that involve the lower half of the half — the jaw and mouth muscles. However, smiles were entirely unique because they involved the eye muscles — the *orbicularis oculi*. These are the muscles that make your eyes squint, such as if you look into a bright light.

Therefore, it was only authentic smiles that were a product of muscle contractions would make the eyes squint. This was called the Duchenne smile.

What is the significance of this?

When someone is smiling, look at their eyes. Are their eyes wide as the moon, or do they appear to be narrowed and smaller than usual? If the eyes appear larger or unaffected, then you are likely dealing with a fake smile. If the eyes are squinting, you've got a Duchenne smile, and are likely dealing with a real smile. It allows you to take a look into people's minds and what they are thinking. We all have fake smiles we use on a daily basis, and if you understand how to dissect real and fake smiles, you can know exactly how you are being received.

You can better understand if people think you are funny, annoying, engaging, or obnoxious. A Duchenne smile is a reaction to an emotion, while a fake smile is a conscious choice. Hopefully you are seeing more of the former.

Now that you have this knowledge, it might also be wise to ensure that your fake smiles involve the eyes, lest you also be found out.

Posture

Posture is also a topic where there are universal themes and standards, so to speak. We all know what good and bad posture and body language look like.

Generally, bad posture is when you appear to be shrinking so people can't see you and will ignore you. This is the type of posture we have when the teacher is looking for someone to call on, yet we don't know the answer. These are universal signs for discomfort and anxiety, and even if you are feeling these inside, you should make an effort to conceal them.

Generally, good posture is when you appear to be standing tall, proud, and unafraid of attention. This is the type of posture we have when we are pretending to be a superhero surveying the land. Your shoulders are back, your chest is puffed out, and your chin is up, almost as if you were looking down your nose at others.

Flex your shoulder blades so they nearly touch

and hold your arms loose at your sides. This is all going to feel unnatural and like you're displaying your cleavage, at first, but take a look in the mirror and look at how much better you look just by standing up straight. As Cuddy's study demonstrated, when you assume powerful body language, you tend to speak more loudly, project better, and use bigger and more powerful gestures. If you feel defeated or small inside, you can simply physically project the opposite and *change your reality*.

You'll smile confidently and engage others because of the positive feedback you'll gain from them. These are the hallmarks of acting charismatic, and your mind will believe the physical reality you've created for yourself. Everything you might imagine a powerful CEO, cowboy, or whoever your idea of a powerful person would do in regards to their posture, that's who you should try to channel or emulate.

No fidgeting is allowed, and you should be wary of crossing your arms and legs because it is often a move to signify your need to feel more protected and safe.

Eye Contact

Much has been written about eye contact already, and not just by me.

Eye contact is the simple ability to look into someone's eyes and hold their gaze. Studies have shown that eye contact actually appears to consume brainpower, and thus it is healthy to not always maintain it (Phelps, 2006).

Other studies have concluded the simple absence of eye contact denoted a lack of trustworthiness (Kreysa, 2016), yet anything over three seconds started to become something resembling psychopathic behavior (Binetti, 2016).

We also know eye contact is important for feeling intimacy and other deep emotions, and we don't need studies to tell us that. It's an essential part of the most powerful types of interpersonal connection. Additional studies showed that when we stop looking at something or someone, we literally stop thinking about them.

So, what do we do with all of this information?

First, we recognize the power and importance of eye contact and pledge to use it more frequently and for no less than one second.

Second, we realize it's the non-verbal equivalent of saying, "Hi, how are you?" which we would never skip when meeting a stranger.

Third, we must treat it as a non-verbal statement of, "I am trustworthy and will probably not slit your throat later," which means people need to feel safe and secure around you.

And finally, if we don't meet people's gaze or we are caught peering around the room, they will do the same and literally stop thinking about us.

It can be uncomfortable, and even stressful to emphasize, but if you meet the minimum requirements for eye contact, all of the aforementioned will be rectified.

Social Touch

The majority of people, if they do not actively crave *social touching*, use it as a proxy for rapport and connection. If you have ever spent time in crowded public transportation, you might have drawn the opposite conclusion, but that's not social touching.

The truth is touching others communicates a level

of intimacy and comfort. It communicates in no uncertain terms that you accept somebody and don't reject them on some level — which, of course, is the same reason we don't want to be touched by strangers on the subway.

When you look at charismatic figures throughout history, you will notice that a lot of them press the flesh. They shake hands, hug people, and are at ease physically interacting with others. This is not just for show. If done right, social touching will not creep out members of the opposite or same sex.

It's just a way to non-verbally show your charismatic presence and sense of welcoming and openness.

The best way to learn social touching (and this is definitely something you should learn and practice first so you can have a clear idea of what to do and what not to do) is to simply observe friends and relatives. When you are with your family and you hug each other and clap each other on the back, you would see what the stated rules are as well as what goes unsaid. Now, extend that to your circle of friends. What are common ways to socially touch friends and acquaintances? Don't underestimate the lessons your friends and relatives are giving you through the way they interact and touch without a second thought — because they are fully at ease. Practice social touching first with your friends and family members. If you drop the ball, the fallout will be practically non-existent. Gradually expand the circle when you can expertly tell what is acceptable in what context.

Give them a hug to say hello, high-five, grab onto their arm to emphasize a point (or your emotional reaction to what they said), or playfully push them if they are sarcastic. Sometimes, all it takes is a hand on the shoulder to physically feel connected and engage someone.

When you touch socially, this physical contact also releases the hormone *oxytocin,* which triggers feelings of intimacy, happiness, and openness. Oxytocin has often been called the love hormone because of how it is released between lovers.

In a 1976 study, workers handed out library cards to patrons with or without briefly touching the hand of the patron. Interviews of the patrons afterwards found that those who were touched, even if they didn't register it consciously, had a more favorable view of the library and worker. Any clue on how this might translate to anyone who relies on a tip for their salary?

A 2011 study conducted by Michael Kraus at the University of Illinois at Urbana-Champaign tracked how often professional basketball players touched each other, such as giving one another high-fives. Touching was highly correlated with team and individual success! No wonder the skin has often been nicknamed "the social organ."

Finally, psychologist Matthew Hertenstein noted in another 2011 study, "With the face and voice, in general we can identify just one or two positive signals that are not confused with each other, but it seems instead that touch is a much more nuanced, sophisticated, and precise way to communicate emotions." In other words, a touch can communicate multiple emotions at once, in more universal and less ambiguous ways.

If communication doesn't hinge on what you say, it certainly means charisma doesn't. It's an accumulation of signals that someone can process about you, and the sum can become greater with each part.

Conclusion

Bill Clinton has taught a few lessons in his day, but the most important to me was the learnable nature of charisma.

By breaking free of the mindset that it is just something that people were born with, it opens up a world of possibilities for anyone seeking to improve themselves. Sure, charisma can appear effortless, and at times incredible, but 99.99% of the time it's a product of years of learning and practice. After all, a marathon seems impossible if you're a couch potato.

Everyone starts somewhere, and curiosity, warmth, and presence are all learnable qualities. It's my hope that you've taken something that you can instantly put into use from this book, and many longer-term strategies for growth.

As for Bill? Well, it's a miracle that I've gotten through this entire book without making a Monica Lewinsky joke.

Sincerely,

Patrick King
Social Interaction Specialist and Conversation Coach
www.PatrickKingConsulting.com

P.S.: If you enjoyed this book, please don't be shy and drop me a line, leave a review, or both! I love reading feedback, and reviews are the lifeblood of Kindle books, so they are always welcome and greatly appreciated.

Speaking and Coaching

Imagine going far beyond the contents of this book and dramatically improving the way you interact with the world and the relationships you'll build.

Are you interested in contacting Patrick for:

- A social skills workshop for your workplace
- Speaking engagements on the power of conversation and charisma
- Personalized social skills and conversation coaching

Patrick speaks around the world to help people improve their lives through the power of building relationships with improved social skills. He is a recognized industry expert, bestselling author, and speaker.

To invite Patrick to speak at your next event or to inquire about coaching, get in touch directly through his website's contact form at http://www.PatrickKingConsulting.com/contact, or contact him directly at Patrick@patrickkingconsulting.com.

Cheat Sheet

Chapter 1. Charisma Deconstructed

Charisma is an eminently learnable quality, and isn't something people were just born with. My preferred definition is that it just measures the ability to have people like you.

Chapter 2. Devote Your Attention

You cannot be charismatic if you don't give your full focus and attention to others. You must undertake the task of creating a world where only the two of you exist.

Chapter 3. Show Your Confidence

Show your power, confidence, and individuality, and make yourself someone people want to be around.

Chapter 4. Exude True Warmth

Learning empathy and how to truly walk in other people's shoes is difficult, but necessary. It will instantly allow you to understand people's emotional states better.

Chapter 5. Choose a Role Model

Choose a charisma role model to emulate and look up to. This will help you in a bind because you can view it like wearing an empowering mask.

Chapter 6. Be a Role Model

Make yourself a role model that other people can admire and aspire to be by displaying positivity, strength, generosity, and charm.

Chapter 7. Shine Your Spotlight

Make people feel special and important with optimal compliments and reactions that let them know you are listening.

Chapter 8. Goal Alignment

Many people have the goal of being charming or charismatic, and that leads them to failure, because our goals can determine our actions in negative ways. Instead, internalize the goal of building trust, comfort, and entertainment.

Chapter 9. Speak Their Language

Try to speak people's language and otherwise reduce the amount of psychological barriers between others to be more easily understood and trusted.

Chapter 10. Charisma No-Nos

Sometimes, it is just as important to remove the negatives as it is to improve anything. People will read the cues they get from you and react accordingly, for better or worse.

Chapter 11. Quickness and Violations

These interesting psychological phenomena are what make people appear charming, and what makes people laugh. We prefer speed over accuracy, and we prefer a benign moral violation.

Chapter 12. Effective Listening

Effective listening is about forgetting your priorities and role, emphasizing the speaker, reflecting, and listening with intent to help.

Chapter 13. It's Not What You Say

Body language is the majority of communication any way you slice it. To this end, your eye contact, facial expressiveness, posture, smiles, and use of social touch have a great impact on how you will are perceived.

Made in the USA
Lexington, KY
07 July 2017